I0473899

Pandemic Influenza Preparedness and Response Guidance for
Healthcare Workers and Healthcare Employers

Occupational Safety and Health Administration
U.S. Department of Labor

OSHA 3328-05R
2009

This document is not a standard or regulation, and it creates no new legal obligations. Likewise, it cannot and does not diminish any obligations established by Federal or state statute, rule or standard. The document is advisory in nature, informational in content, and is intended to assist employers in providing a safe and healthful workplace. *The Occupational Safety and Health Act* requires employers to comply with hazard-specific safety and health standards. In addition, pursuant to Section 5(a)(1), the General Duty Clause of the Act, employers must provide their employees with a workplace free from recognized hazards likely to cause death or serious physical harm. Employers can be cited for violating the General Duty Clause if there is a recognized hazard and they do not take reasonable steps to prevent or abate the hazard.

ACRONYMS

CDC	Centers for Disease Control and Prevention
EPA	U.S. Environmental Protection Agency
HEPA	high-efficiency particulate air
HHS	U.S. Department of Health and Human Services
JCAHO	Joint Commission on Accreditation of Healthcare Organizations
LRN	Laboratory Response Network
NIOSH	National Institute for Occupational Safety and Health
OSH Act	Occupational Safety and Health Act of 1970
OSHA	Occupational Safety and Health Administration
PAPR	powered air-purifying respirator
PLHCP	physician or another licensed healthcare professional
PPE	personal protective equipment
RT-PCR	reverse transcriptase polymerase chain reaction
SARS	severe acute respiratory syndrome
SNS	Strategic National Stockpile
SPN	Sentinel Provider Network
WHO	World Health Organization

Contents

Introduction

A pandemic is a global disease outbreak. A flu pandemic occurs when a new influenza virus emerges for which people have little or no immunity, and for which there is no vaccine. The disease spreads easily person-to-person, causes serious illness, and can sweep across the country and around the world in a very short time.

It is difficult to predict when the next influenza pandemic will occur or how severe it will be. Wherever and whenever a pandemic starts, everyone around the world is at risk. Countries might, through measures such as border closures and travel restrictions, delay arrival of the virus, but they cannot stop it.

An especially severe influenza pandemic could lead to high levels of illness, death, social disruption, and economic loss. Everyday life would be disrupted because so many people in so many places become seriously ill at the same time. Impacts can range from school and business closings to the interruption of basic services such as public transportation and food delivery.

An influenza pandemic is projected to have a global impact on morbidity and mortality, thus requiring a sustained, large-scale response from the healthcare community. The 1918 influenza pandemic was responsible for over 500,000 deaths in the United States, while the 1957 and 1968 pandemic influenza viruses were responsible for 70,000 and 34,000 deaths, respectively.[1] More recently, one modeling study estimated that an influenza pandemic affecting 15 to 35 percent of the United States population could cause 89,000 to 207,000 deaths, 314,000 to 734,000 hospitalizations, 18 to 42 million outpatient visits, and 20 to 47 million additional illnesses.[2] In contrast, from 1990 to 1999, seasonal influenza caused approximately 36,000 deaths per year in the United States.[3]

A substantial percentage of the world's population will require some form of medical care. Healthcare facilities can be overwhelmed, creating a shortage of hospital staff, beds, ventilators and other supplies. Surge capacity at non-traditional sites such as schools may need to be created to cope with the demand.

It is expected that such an event will quickly overwhelm the healthcare system locally, regionally, and nationally.[4] An increased number of sick individuals will seek healthcare services. In addition, the number of healthcare workers available to respond to these increased demands will be reduced by illness rates similar to pandemic influenza attack rates affecting the rest of the population. Finally, healthcare workers and healthcare resources will also be expected to continue to meet non-pandemic associated healthcare needs.

In order to mitigate the effects of an influenza pandemic on the healthcare community, it is important to identify healthcare providers and recognize the diversity of practice settings.

- The delivery of healthcare services requires a broad range of employees, such as first responders, nurses, physicians, pharmacists, technicians and aides, building maintenance, security and administrative personnel, social workers, laboratory employees, food service, housekeeping, and mortuary personnel. Moreover, these employees can be found in a variety of workplace settings, including hospitals, chronic care facilities, outpatient clinics (e.g., medical and dental offices, schools, physical and rehabilitation therapy centers, health departments, occupational health clinics, and prisons), free-standing ambulatory care and surgical facilities, and emergency response settings.

- The diversity among healthcare workers and their workplaces makes preparation and response to a pandemic influenza especially challenging. For example, not all employees in the same healthcare facility will have the same risk of acquiring influenza, not all individuals with the same job title will have the same risk of infection, and not all healthcare facilities will be at equal risk although all will be similarly susceptible. During an influenza pandemic, healthcare workers may be required to provide services in newly established healthcare facilities to accommodate patient overflow from traditional healthcare settings (e.g., convention centers, schools, and sports arenas). Consequently, the cornerstone of pandemic influenza preparedness and response is an assessment of risk and the development of effective policies and procedures tailored to the unique aspects of various healthcare settings.

Collaboration with state and federal partners is vital to ensure that healthcare workers are adequately protected during an influenza pandemic. The goal of this document is to help healthcare workers and employers prepare for and respond to an influenza pandemic.

The guidance document is organized into four major sections:
- Clinical background information on influenza

- Infection control
- Pandemic influenza preparedness
- OSHA standards of special importance

Given the technical nature and breadth of information available in the document, each section has been subdivided (see Table of Contents) in order to allow readers to quickly focus on areas of interest.

The document also contains appendices which provide pandemic planners with samples of infection control plans, examples of practical pandemic planning tools and additional technical information. Topic areas include Internet resources, communication tools, sample infection control programs, self-triage and home care resources, diagnosis and treatment of staff during a pandemic, planning and supply checklists and risk communication. This educational material has been provided for informational purposes only and should be used in conjunction with the entire document in order to ensure that healthcare workers are adequately protected during a pandemic. OSHA does not recommend one option over the many effective alternatives that exist.

OSHA has prepared additional, general information to assist workplaces in their preparation for an influenza pandemic entitled, *Guidance on Preparing Workplaces for an Influenza Pandemic* which is available at www.osha.gov.

References

[1] U.S. Department of Health and Human Services (HHS). Pandemicflu.gov, General Information. Last accessed June 7, 2006: http://www.pandemicflu.gov/general/.

[2] Meltzer M.I., N.J. Cox, K. Fukuda. 1999. The economic impact of pandemic influenza in the United States: priorities for intervention. Emerg Infect Dis 5:659-71.

[3] Thompson W.W., D.K. Shay, E. Weintraub, et al. 2003. Mortality associated with influenza and respiratory syncytial virus in the United States. JAMA 289:179-86.

[4] Waldhorn R., E. Toner. 2005. Challenges to hospital medical preparedness and response in a flu pandemic. Center for Biosecurity, University of Pittsburgh Medical Center. October 12, 2005. Last accessed June 7, 2006: http://www.upmc-biosecurity.org/avianflu/facts-hospitalprep.html

Influenza: Clinical Background Information

Historically, influenza has caused outbreaks of respiratory illness for centuries, including three pandemics (worldwide outbreaks of disease) in the 20th century.[1] There are three types of influenza viruses: types A, B, and C. Only type A influenza viruses cause pandemics. Seasonal influenza outbreaks can be caused by either type A or type B influenza viruses. Influenza type C viruses cause mild illness in humans but do not cause epidemics or pandemics. This guidance is aimed at protecting healthcare workers in the event of an influenza pandemic; therefore, the focus will be on the characteristics of type A influenza viruses.

Of the three types of influenza viruses, only type A is divided into subtypes. Subtype designations are based on the presence of two viral surface proteins (antigens): hemagglutinin (H) and neuraminidase (N). To date, 16 different hemagglutinin and 9 different neuraminidase surface proteins have been identified in influenza A viruses.[2] Subtypes are designated as the H protein type (1–16) solely or followed by the N protein type (1–9) (e.g., H5N1). Three different subtypes (i.e., H1N1, H2N2, and H3N2) have caused pandemics in the 20th century. Influenza A viruses vary in virulence, infectivity to specific hosts, modes of transmission, and the clinical presentation of infection.

Seasonal, avian, and pandemic influenza can occur in humans. It is important to have a basic understanding of the terms seasonal, avian and pandemic influenza in order to appreciate the guidance in this document.

- **Seasonal influenza** or "flu" refers to periodic outbreaks of acute onset viral respiratory infection caused by circulating strains of human influenza A and B viruses. Seasonal "flu" is the kind of influenza with which healthcare workers and the public are most familiar. In temperate regions of the world, seasonal influenza generally occurs most frequently during the winter months when the humidity and outdoor temperatures are low (generally from December until April in northern temperate regions). Between 5–20 percent of the population may be infected annually. Most people have some immunity to the currently circulating strains of influenza virus and, as a result, the severity and impact of seasonal influenza is substantially less than during pandemics. Each year, a trivalent influenza vaccine is prepared in advance of the anticipated seasonal outbreak and it includes those strains (two type A and one type B) that are expected to be the most likely to circulate in the upcoming "flu" season. Influenza vaccine is currently targeted toward those at greatest risk of influenza-related complications and their contacts, such as healthcare workers.

- **Avian influenza**, also known as the bird flu, is caused by type A influenza viruses that infect wild birds and domestic poultry. Some forms of the avian influenza are worse than others. Avian influenza viruses are generally divided into two groups: low pathogenic avian influenza and highly pathogenic avian influenza. Low pathogenic avian influenza naturally occurs in wild birds and can spread to domestic birds. In most cases it causes no signs of infection or only minor symptoms in birds. In general, these low pathogenic strains of the virus pose little threat to human health. Low pathogenic avian influenza virus H5 and H7 strains have the potential to mutate into highly pathogenic avian influenza and are, therefore, closely monitored. Highly pathogenic avian influenza spreads rapidly and has a high death rate in birds. Highly pathogenic avian influenza of the H5N1 strain is rapidly spreading in birds in some parts of the world.

Highly pathogenic H5N1 is one of the few avian influenza viruses to have crossed the species barrier to infect humans, and it is the most deadly of those that have crossed the barrier. Most cases of highly pathogenic H5N1 infection in humans have resulted from contact with infected poultry or surfaces contaminated with secretion/excretions from infected birds.

As of November 2006, the spread of highly pathogenic H5N1 avian influenza virus from person to person has been limited to rare, sporadic cases. Nonetheless, because all influenza viruses have the ability to change, scientists are concerned that highly pathogenic H5N1 avian influenza virus one day could be able to sustain human-to-human transmission. Because these viruses do not commonly infect humans, there is little or no immune protection against them in the human population. If the highly pathogenic H5N1 avian influenza virus were to gain the capacity to sustain transmission from person to person, a pandemic could begin.

- **Pandemic influenza** refers to a global disease outbreak. A flu pandemic occurs when a new influenza type A virus emerges for which people have little or no immunity, and for which there is no vaccine. The disease spreads easily person-to-person, causes serious illness, and can sweep across the country and around the world in a very short time. Such a virus is likely to have origins from avian viruses or possibly from other animal sources (e.g., pigs). Many scientists believe that since no pandemic has occurred since 1968, it is only a matter of time before another pandemic occurs. A pandemic may occur in waves of outbreaks with each wave in a community lasting 8 to 12 weeks. One-to-three waves may occur.

Rapid detection of unusual influenza outbreaks, isolation of possible pandemic viruses and the immediate notification of national and international health authorities is critical for mounting a timely and effective response to a potential pandemic. The World Health Organization (WHO) maintains a global surveillance system of circulating influenza strains and a *Global Influenza Preparedness Plan*.[3] The WHO Plan describes six phases of increasing public health risk associated with the emergence of a new influenza virus subtype that may pose a pandemic threat. The WHO bases alerts on these six different phases.

The first two phases of the WHO Pandemic Alert System comprise the "Inter-pandemic Period" in which there is a novel influenza A virus in animals, but no human cases have been observed. Phase 2 indicates that an animal influenza subtype that poses a risk to humans has been detected. The next three phases (Phases 3–5) compose the "Pandemic Alert Period" in which a novel influenza virus causes human infection with a new subtype, but does not exhibit efficient and sustained human-to-human transmission. Once a new influenza A virus develops the capacity for efficient and sustained human-to-human transmission in the general population (Phase 6), the WHO declares that an influenza pandemic is in progress (this is known as the "Pandemic Period").

For additional information visit WHO's Epidemic and Pandemic Alert and Response website at http://www.who.int/csr/disease/avian_influenza/phase/en/index.html. Federal government response stages to these WHO phases are described in the National Strategy for Pandemic Influenza: Implementation Plan which can be found at http:// www.whitehouse.gov/ homeland/pandemic influenza-implementation.html.

Clinical Presentation of Influenza

It may be useful for healthcare providers to be aware of the clinical presentation of seasonal influenza, prior influenza pandemics, and highly pathogenic avian influenza in humans to assist them when evaluating patients who present with influenza-like illness.

The clinical picture of influenza infections can vary from no symptoms at all in seasonal influenza to fulminant (fully symptomatic) disease in pandemic strains that result in severe illness and death, even among previously healthy adults and children.[4] Fever and respiratory symptoms are characteristic of all forms of influenza. The Centers for Disease Control and Prevention's (CDC's) Sentinel Provider Network (SPN) monitors influenza timing and severity. The SPN[5] is comprised of approximately 2,300 primary care providers that provide weekly reports on outpatient "influenza-like illnesses" to state health departments and to the CDC. The SPN uses "fever >100° F or 37.8° C and sore throat and/or cough in the absence of a known cause other than influenza" as its definition of influenza-like illness.

Clinical Presentation of Seasonal Influenza
Seasonal influenza typically has an abrupt onset, with symptoms of fever, chills, fatigue, muscle aches, headache, dry cough, upper respiratory congestion, and sore throat.[6] The time from exposure to disease onset is usually 1 to 4 days, with an average of 2 days. Most patients recover within 3 to 7 days.[7] In adults, fevers usually last for 2 to 3 days, but may last longer in children. Cough and weakness can persist for up to 2 weeks. Except for fever, the physical examination has few specific findings. Typically there is weakness and mild inflammation of the upper respiratory tract. Routine outpatient laboratory findings are also non-specific. Available laboratory tests that are specific for influenza are described in the Diagnosis section on page 9 of this document.

Adults are possibly infectious from about 1 day before until about 5 days after the onset of clinical illness. Children and the immunocompromised (e.g., people with HIV infection, organ transplantation or receiving chronic steroids) have a much longer period of infectivity. Children can be infectious for 10 or more days, and young children can shed the virus for several days before the onset of illness. Severely immunocompromised persons can shed the virus for weeks or months.[7]

Seasonal influenza is responsible for approximately 36,000 deaths and 226,000 hospitalizations annually in the United States.[8] The risk of death is highest among the elderly, the very young, and patients with cardiopulmonary and other chronic conditions.[7]

Clinical Presentations of Prior Influenza Pandemics

The 1918 influenza pandemic, caused by subtype H1N1 viruses, had signs and symptoms of far greater severity than seasonal influenza. It resulted in death for an estimated 500,000 U.S. citizens and as many as 40 million people worldwide. The 1918 pandemic disproportionately affected young, healthy adults, between the ages of 15 and 35. A significant proportion of patients developed fulminant disease, accompanied by a striking perioral cyanosis, leading to death within a few days. Postmortem examinations in these patients frequently revealed denuding tracheobronchitis, pulmonary hemorrhage, or pulmonary edema. Others survived the initial illness, only to die of a secondary bacterial pneumonia.[6]

The 1957 (caused by subtype H2N2 viruses) and 1968 (caused by subtype H3N2 viruses) influenza pandemics killed an estimated 70,000 and 34,000 U.S. citizens, respectively.[8] The clinical features of the pandemics of 1957 and 1968 were also typical of influenza-like illness, including fever, chills, headache, sore throat, malaise, cough, and coryza, but were milder compared to the 1918–19 pandemic.[6] The 1957 influenza pandemic was notable for severe complications, such as primary viral pneumonia, particularly in pregnant women. As in the pandemic of 1918, some people survived the initial viral infection, only to later die of a secondary bacterial pneumonia.

Clinical Presentation of Highly Pathogenic Avian Influenza in Humans

The highly pathogenic H5N1 avian influenza virus that caused outbreaks in Hong Kong, Thailand, Vietnam, and Cambodia, like the 1918 pandemic virus, primarily resulted in disease in children and young adults.[9] Hospitalized patients initially developed typical seasonal influenza symptoms such as high fever and cough, but unlike seasonal influenza, there were lower respiratory tract rather than upper respiratory tract symptoms. Because of the involvement of the lower respiratory tract, patients typically had shortness of breath and almost all patients had developed viral pneumonia at the time of hospitalization. Also unlike typical seasonal influenza, diarrhea, abdominal pain, and vomiting were frequently reported. Common laboratory findings were lymphopenia, thrombocytopenia and elevated aminotransferase levels.

As of November 13, 2006, highly pathogenic H5N1 viruses had not been detected in animals or humans in the United States. For up-to-date information regarding the number of human cases of avian influenza and deaths worldwide, visit the WHO Confirmed Cases of Human Influenza A (H5N1) website at http://www.who.int/csr/disease/avian_influenza/country/en/.

An outbreak of another avian influenza virus, H7N7, occurred among poultry farm employees and those helping to contain the outbreak in the Netherlands in 2003.[10] The clinical course of this influenza virus was unusual in that conjunctivitis was a common finding and fewer affected persons had respiratory symptoms, although the one fatality among the 89 human cases was associated with respiratory disease. No further outbreaks were reported through April 24, 2006 (http://www.cdc.gov/flu/avian/gen-info/avian-flu-humans.htm).

Diagnosis

Accurate and timely influenza diagnosis requires knowledge of the likely clinical presentations of seasonal influenza and of any circulating strains of novel viral subtypes, an awareness of the risks for exposure, and knowledge of the capabilities and limitations of laboratory diagnostic tests.

The more quickly a new pandemic virus can be identified, the sooner actions can be taken to isolate the initial cases and initiate other public health measures to prevent spread through the community *and* the sooner infection control measures can be implemented to protect the community's healthcare workers.

Clinical Diagnosis of Seasonal Influenza

Uncomplicated seasonal influenza presents as a sudden onset of fever and respiratory illness with muscle aches, headaches, nonproductive cough, sore throat, and runny nose. Children can also have ear infections and/or gastrointestinal symptoms.[7] The diagnosis of the influenzas will be primarily through recognizing symptom complexes such as those used in surveillance. The SPN definition for influenza-like illness is used for seasonal influenza surveillance.[5] However, this definition is not specific and may share features with other respiratory illnesses present in the community.

The likelihood of a clinical sign or symptom to accurately detect influenza infection in a group of patients is called sensitivity. Conversely, the likelihood of a clinical sign or symptom to exclude influenza infection in a group of patients who do not have influenza is called specificity. Both the sensitivity and specificity of clinical signs and symptoms of influenza infection vary with multiple factors, including patient age, vaccination status, hospitalization status, degree of co-circulation of other infectious agents that cause respiratory symptoms in the community, and the percentage of the population infected with influenza (prevalence). The clinical signs and symptoms of influenza have been studied using viral cultures as the criteria for definitive influenza diagnosis in groups of mostly young adults when influenza was circulating in their community. It has been reported that the use of the influenza-like case definition is 63 to 78% accurate in identifying culture-confirmed cases of influenza (a sensitivity of 63 to 78%) and 55 to 71% accurate in excluding influenza (specificity of 55 to 71%).[7] The sensitivity and specificity will vary based on the percentage of all respiratory illnesses that are due to influenza. Other studies have addressed influenza signs and symptoms in different groups.[11, 12]

There is considerable overlap in the clinical presentation of seasonal influenza and other viral and bacterial respiratory infections. Influenza surveillance case definitions and laboratory testing can assist in differentiating among these infections. However, clinicians must always maintain a level of awareness that co-infections with bacterial respiratory infections or non-influenza viruses can occur with seasonal influenza. Clinical judgment regarding diagnosis and treatment is needed in conjunction with laboratory testing in order to differentiate between potential infectious organisms.

Laboratory Diagnosis of Seasonal Influenza

During Inter-pandemic and Pandemic Alert Periods, use of laboratory diagnostic tests for influenza supports seasonal influenza surveillance and provides laboratory detection of novel influenza subtypes. There are multiple laboratory techniques for identifying influenza viruses, including the rapid antigen test, the reverse transcriptase polymerase chain reaction (RT-PCR) assays, virus isolation, and immunofluorescence antibody assays.[13]

When respiratory secretions are used for seasonal influenza diagnosis, nasopharyngeal samples are more likely to yield a positive result than are pharyngeal swab samples.[14] Commercial rapid testing can detect influenza virus in less than 30 minutes. However, some of these tests are not very sensitive[9] (false negative results are common) and not all of these tests are able to distinguish between influenza A and B viruses (see Safety Tips for Laboratorians: Cautions in Using Rapid Tests for Influenza A Viruses at http://www.fda.gov/cdrh/oivd/tips/rapidflu.html). When influenza is suspected during an outbreak of respiratory illness, both rapid testing and viral cultures should be done. Although viral cultures require five days or more to perform, they can provide specific information on the strain

and subtype of the influenza virus tested, and provide information on the sensitivity to antiviral medication as well.[14] The HHS/CDC Influenza (Flu) Laboratory Diagnostic Procedures for Influenza website (http://www.cdc.gov/flu/professionals/labdiagnosis.htm) maintains a table of the available diagnostic tests for the influenza virus.[14]

Clinical Diagnosis of Pandemic Influenza

Patients with pandemic influenza will likely have clinical signs and symptoms similar to seasonal influenza, although the clinical presentation and course of illness may be severe in a higher percentage of the cases of pandemic influenza. In general, if the next pandemic is comparable to the 1918 Type A H1N1 virus, the pandemic influenza is likely to be far more severe than seasonal influenza, and might disproportionately affect a younger population.

An important factor to look for when evaluating patients for the presence of pandemic influenza during all phases of a WHO Pandemic Alert Period, when human infection with a new subtype is detected, is a possible source of exposure. For instance, the current sources of exposure to highly pathogenic H5N1, the avian influenza virus of most concern, would likely involve international travel or occupational exposure to infected poultry or wild birds. Emergency room physicians and other healthcare personnel interviewing patients with influenza-like illness should ask about recent travel history.

A patient who has a history of travel to a country affected by a novel influenza virus and who has the onset of influenza-like illness within the known incubation period for that virus should be suspected to be infected with the novel influenza virus. Seasonal influenza incubation is usually 1 to 4 days, but novel influenza viruses may have longer incubation periods, possibly up to 10 days.[6] A frequently updated report of countries that have had human infections with highly pathogenic H5N1 avian influenza viruses is available at the WHO Web website at http://www.who.int/csr/disease/avianinfluenza/en/.

Individuals who handle or process animals with a novel virus, laboratory personnel who analyze specimens containing a novel virus and healthcare workers who care for patients infected with a novel virus are at risk for contracting that viral infection. If the virus of concern has not yet been shown to be capable of sustained human-to-human transmission, occupational risk would be higher for employees with exposure to animal or animal products.[6]

Laboratory Diagnosis of Avian and Pandemic Influenza

Currently, the highly pathogenic H5N1 avian influenza virus is considered to have the greatest potential for mutation to a pandemic virus given how widespread the virus is and because it has already caused illness and death in people. This virus has spread rapidly in bird populations throughout Asia, Europe, and Africa. Recently, HHS/CDC developed a 4-hour RT-PCR assay for the detection of the gene coding for the H5 surface protein of the Asian lineage of the highly pathogenic H5N1 avian influenza virus.[15] These RT-PCR reagents have been distributed to approximately 140 designated laboratories of the Laboratory Response Network (LRN) which has laboratories located in all 50 states.[15] The RT-PCR testing should be done when a patient has severe respiratory illness and clinical or epidemiological risk. Clinicians should contact their local or state health department as soon as possible to report any suspected human case of influenza H5N1 in the United States. Positive tests for influenza A H5N1 in the United States should be confirmed by HHS/CDC, which has been designated as a WHO H5 Reference laboratory. An HHS/CDC guidance document *Updated Interim Guidance for Laboratory Testing of Persons with Suspected Infection with Avian Influenza A (H5N1) Virus in the United States* is distributed via the Health Alert Network (HAN) at http://www2a.cdc.gov/han/ArchiveSys/ViewMsgV.asp?AlertNum=00246. Tests for other avian viruses with pandemic potential are also being developed.

Modes of Transmission

Information on the mode of seasonal influenza transmission is based on previous influenza outbreaks. However, the transmission characteristics of a pandemic influenza virus will not be known until after the pandemic begins. This section covers the transmission patterns of seasonal influenza and past and potential pandemic influenza outbreaks.

Seasonal Influenza Transmission

The usual method of seasonal influenza transmission is assumed to be through coughs and sneezes of infected persons within close proximity. A susceptible person may develop symptoms within 1 to 4 days after exposure to an infected patient who is shedding the influenza virus. The newly infected person is then infectious for about 6 days, usually beginning 1 day prior to the onset of symptoms. This varies with age and disease, as discussed previously.

The relative importance of the various routes of transmission is not known, although it is now commonly accepted that the spread of seasonal influenza requires close proximity—via exposure to large droplets (droplet transmission), direct contact (contact transmission), or near range exposure to aerosols.[16] The term "near range" is used to differentiate influenza airborne transmission from the long-range airborne transmission seen in diseases such as tuberculosis, where disease spread can occur over long distances and prolonged periods of time.

Droplet Transmission

Epidemiologic patterns suggest that droplet transmission is a major route of influenza spread. Susceptible individuals are subject to infection by large particle droplets from infected patients. Droplets are produced by coughing, sneezing, or talking, or by therapeutic manipulations such as suctioning or bronchoscopy. Infected droplets may enter the susceptible individual through the conjunctiva of the eye or the mucus membranes of the mouth or nose. Droplets travel only about 3 feet and do not remain in the air, so special ventilation procedures and advanced respiratory protection is not required to prevent this type of transmission.[16]

Airborne Transmission

Airborne transmission, as occurs in tuberculosis, is spread through small infectious particles such as droplet nuclei.[17] Unlike the larger droplets, these very small airborne droplet nuclei can be readily disseminated by air currents to susceptible individuals. They can travel significant distances and can penetrate deep into the lung to the alveoli where they can establish an infection. The presence of significant airborne transmission would indicate the need for ventilation procedures and respiratory protection greater than that afforded by a surgical mask, e.g., a NIOSH-certified N95 or higher respirator.

No study has definitively established airborne transmission as a major route of influenza transmission, but multiple studies suggest that some airborne influenza transmission may occur. Experiments in mice have demonstrated that air exchange can decrease influenza virus transmission, and have demonstrated infectious particles that are smaller than ten microns.[18] A ferret study demonstrated that influenza virus transmission can occur through a vent with right angles. A human volunteer study demonstrated that, when a small droplet aerosol is used, influenza transmission can occur with lower virus concentrations.[19] Another human observational study documented the spread of influenza to 72 percent of the passengers and crew on an airplane with a ventilation system that was not functioning for 3 hours.[20] While these studies suggest that airborne influenza transmission occurs under certain conditions, the proportion of influenza illness resulting from this route of transmission is unknown.

Contact Transmission

Contact transmission can be direct or indirect. Direct contact transmission occurs by touching skin to skin, usually during direct patient care activities such as turning or bathing patients, or by shaking hands. Indirect transmission occurs when infected material from the patient is deposited in the environment and is taken up by a susceptible individual.[16]

There is limited data on the survivability of influenza A and B viruses outside of the human host. One study,[21] conducted by Bean et al., suggests that that if a heavily infected person contaminated a stainless steel surface, there might be enough viable viral particles remaining after 2-8 hours to allow contact transmission to a susceptible person. It should be noted that this study was conducted at a relative humidity of 35 to 40 percent, a level that favors the survival of influenza viruses. Other studies have clearly demonstrated that humidity plays a significant role in influenza viral survival with survival times being longer at lower humidity.

Further research is needed to more fully appreciate the role of contact transmission for various strains of influenza and the effect of varying environmental conditions. Although it is assumed that influenza spreads by contact transmission, the proportion of spread that occurs through this mechanism is unknown.[16]

Pandemic Influenza Transmission

This section discusses observational studies on human-to-human transmission during previous influenza pandemics and observations about implications for transmission of current avian influenza virus infections that are of concern for possible future influenza pandemics.

Transmission, Past Pandemics

One influenza transmission study conducted during the 1957 pandemic indicated the importance of person-to-person spread while another suggested the apparent importance of airborne transmission. The first study, an epidemiological study demonstrated

influenza transmission from a newly hospitalized, infected patient who had no isolation precautions to three healthcare workers and one adjacent patient. Ultimately, 30 of the 62 exposed patients and ward staff became ill.[22] Although the authors did not address the likely mode of transmission, a later analysis of the data was interpreted as not consistent with a single source pattern as would be seen in airborne transmission.[17] The second study, an observational influenza transmission study during the 1957 pandemic conducted at a Veterans Administration Hospital suggested airborne transmission. The study compared the influenza illness rates in tuberculosis patients in wards with and without ultraviolet ceiling lights and found rates of 2 percent and 19 percent, respectively. The authors of this study suggest this finding implies that transmission of influenza was significantly blocked by radiant (UV) disinfection of droplet nuclei.[23]

Transmission, Possible Future Pandemics

The influenza viruses that are currently of greatest concern for possible future pandemics are the highly pathogenic avian influenza viruses, most notably strains of H5N1 and H7N7, which have caused outbreaks among humans.

A summary of the clinical features of hospitalized patients with highly pathogenic H5N1 avian influenza described a clinical course that differed from seasonal influenzas. The highly pathogenic H5N1 avian influenza had an initial presentation with *lower* respiratory tract symptoms and viral pneumonia (seasonal influenzas present more often with upper respiratory symptoms), a higher ribonucleic acid detection in *pharyngeal* samples (seasonal influenzas have higher viral detection in *nasal* samples), and more frequent diarrhea, abdominal pain, and vomiting. The detection of infectious virus and ribonucleic acid in the blood, cerebrospinal fluid (CSF) and feces of one patient, a child,[9] raises concern that transmission of this virus may be possible by contact with blood, CSF and feces in addition to respiratory secretions, but this remains unknown.

An outbreak of highly pathogenic H7N7 avian influenza virus occurred in poultry farm employees in the Netherlands in 2003.[10] This influenza's clinical course was unique in that it was mainly associated with conjunctivitis. Seasonal influenza transmission is considered to take place primarily through the respiratory tract, but the conjunctivitis component of highly pathogenic H7N7 avian influenza suggests that its transmission may also occur via the mucous membranes of the eye.

Treatment and Prevention

Treatment and prevention of influenza involves multiple infection control measures, including vaccination, antiviral medications, and management of influenza complications. This section concentrates on immunization and antiviral medications.

Seasonal Influenza Treatment and Prevention

Medications available for influenza A treatment and prophylaxis include the M2 ion channel inhibitors (also known as adamantanes) amantadine and rimantadine and the neuraminidase inhibitors zanamivir and oseltamivir. Presently, only the neuraminidase inhibitors are available for treatment and prophylaxis of *both* influenza A and B. Current HHS/CDC drug recommendations, announced during the 2005-2006 influenza season (see http://www.cdc.gov/flu/han011406.htm), advise against the use of adamantanes for seasonal influenza due to resistance. Therefore, the neuraminidase inhibitors oseltamivir and zanamivir are the only drugs currently recommended for treatment and prophylaxis of influenza. Neuraminidase inhibitors are prescription drugs and they are most effective for treatment when use begins within two days of symptom onset. Clinicians should adhere to HHS/CDC recommendations regarding the use of antivirals.[24]

Antiviral medications can be used to prevent influenza, but the primary strategy for preventing influenza infections is vaccination. Vaccines are available in two forms: 1) as an intranasal live attenuated vaccine and 2) as an injectable, inactivated trivalent vaccine. Indications and contraindications differ among the preparations.[25] Annual vaccination has been shown to reduce the incidence of influenza infections in healthcare workers.[25, 26, 27] Infection control measures are another means to prevent infection, but their benefit is less well established.

Pandemic Influenza Treatment and Prevention

The appropriate use of antiviral drugs during a pandemic could reduce mortality and morbidity. At the time of this writing, HHS recommendations for treatment of novel viruses are to use the neuraminidase inhibitors zanamivir and oseltamivir because of influenza resistance to amantadine and rimantadine.[24]

Although the magnitude of drug effect against infections with novel strains cannot be predicted precisely, early use is expected to be important for drug effectiveness. The availability of adequate antiviral supplies during a pandemic is far from certain, and, therefore, the HHS *Pandemic Influenza Plan* provides antiviral drug use priority recommendations. Healthcare workers are included in the priority group recommendations.[28]

A vaccine against a specific pandemic influenza strain will likely not be available until after the pandemic begins. But vaccinations against seasonal influenza during the WHO's Interpandemic and Pandemic Alert Period can reduce co-infections and might ameliorate pandemic effects. HHS recommendations are for enhanced levels of seasonal influenza vaccinations in groups at risk for severe influenza and healthcare workers. In addition, HHS recommends enhanced pneumococcal polysaccharide vaccination for some individuals.[29] A limited amount of H5N1 avian influenza vaccine is being stockpiled. However, as the pandemic virus cannot be predicted, it is unknown if stockpiled vaccine will provide protection against a future circulating pandemic influenza virus. A monovalent vaccine is expected to start becoming available within four-to-six months after identification of a specific pandemic virus strain. As noted above, the HHS *Pandemic Influenza Plan* recommends that healthcare workers be included on the priority list (which has not been fully defined) when the availability of pandemic influenza vaccinations is limited.[28, 29]

References

[1] Murphy B.R., R.G. Webster 1996. Orthomyxoviruses. In Fields Virology. Third Edition. Fields B.N., D.M. Knipe, P.M. Howley, editors. Philadelphia, PA: Lippincott-Raven, New York. pp. 1397-445.

[2] Perdue, M.L., D.E. Swayne. 2005. Public Health Risk from Avian Influenza Viruses. Avian Dis 49:317-327. September.

[3] HHS. 2006. Pandemic Influenza Plan, Appendix C. U.S. Department of Health and Human Services. Last accessed April 12, 2006: http://www.hhs.gov/pandemicflu/plan/appendixc.html.

[4] CDC. 2005. Pandemic Influenza Key Facts. Centers for Disease Control and Prevention. Last accessed June 6, 2006: http://www.cdc.gov/flu/keyfacts.htm.

[5] HHS. 2005. Pandemic Influenza Plan, Supplement 1. U.S. Department of Health and Human Services. Last accessed February 2, 2005: http://www.hhs.gov/pandemicflu/plan/sup1.html.

[6] HHS. 2005. Pandemic Influenza Plan, Supplement 5. U.S. Department of Health and Human Services. Last accessed February 2, 2006: http://www.hhs.gov/pandemicflu/plan/sup5.html.

[7] CDC. 2006. Influenza Clinical Description and Diagnosis. Centers for Disease Control and Prevention. Last accessed February 2, 2006: http://www.cdc.gov/flu/professionals/diagnosis/

[8] HHS. 2005. Pandemic Influenza Plan, Appendix B. U.S. Department of Health and Human Services. Last accessed February 2, 2006: http://www.hhs.gov/pandemicflu/plan/appendixb.html.

[9] Beigel J.H., J. Farrar, A.M. Ham, et al. 2005. Avian influenza A (H5N1) infection in humans. A/H5. N Engl J Med 353(13):1374-85.

[10] Du Ry van Beest Holle M., et al. 2005. Human-to-human transmission of avian influenza A/H7N7, the Netherlands, 2003. Euro Surveill 1;10(12).

[11] Walsh E.E., C. Cox, A.R. Falsey. 2002. Clinical features of influenza A virus infection in older hospitalized persons. J Am Geriatr Soc 50(9):1498-503. September 8.

[12] Monto A.S., S. Gravenstein, M. Elliot, M. Colopy, J. Schweinle. 2000. Clinical signs and symptoms predicting influenza infection. Arch Intern Med 160(21): 3243-7. November 27. Comments in Arch Intern Med 161(10):1351-2.

[13] HHS. 2005. Pandemic Influenza Plan. Supplement 2: Laboratory Diagnostics. U.S. Department of Health and Human Services. Last accessed March 21, 2006: http://www.hhs.gov/pandemicflu/plan/sup2.html.

[14] CDC. 2005. Laboratory Diagnostic Procedures for Influenza. Last accessed March 21, 2006: http://www.cdc.gov/flu/professionals/labdiagnosis.htm.

[15] MMWR. 2006. New laboratory assay for diagnostic testing of avian influenza A/H5. Morbidity and Mortality Weekly Report (MMWR). Last accessed March 21, 2006: http://www.cdc.gov/mmwr/preview/mmwrhtml/mm5505a3.htm.

[16] HHS. 2005. Pandemic Influenza Plan, Supplement 4. U.S. Department of Health and Human Services. Last accessed February 20, 2005: http://www.hhs.gov/pandemicflu/plan/sup4.html.

[17] Bridges C.B., M.J. Kuehnert, C.B. Hall. 2003. Transmission of influenza: implications for control in health care settings. Clin Infect Dis 37(8):1094-1101.

[18] Schulman J.L. 1967. Experimental transmission of influenza virus infection in mice: IV. Relationship of transmissibility of different strains of virus and recovery of airborne virus in the environment of infector mice. J Exp Med 125(3):479-88.

[19] Alford R.H., J.A. Kasel, V. Knight. 1966. Human influenza resulting from aerosol inhalation. Proc Soc Exp Biol Med 122(3):800-804.

[20] Moser M.R., T.R. Bender, H.S. Margolis, G.R. Nobel, A.P. Kendal, D.G. Ritter. 1979. An outbreak of influenza aboard a commercial airliner. Am J Epidemiol 110(1):1-6. July.

[21] Bean, B., B.M. Moore, B. Sterner, L.R. Peterson, D.N. Gerding, H.H. Balfour. 1982. Survival of influenza viruses on environmental surfaces. J Infect Dis 146(1):47-51. July.

[22] Blumenfeld H.L., E.D. Kilbourne, D.B. Louria, D.F. Rogers. 1959. Studies on influenza in the pandemic of 1957-1958. I. An epidemiologic, clinical and serologic investigation of an intrahospital epidemic, with a note on vaccination efficacy. J Clin Invest 38(1 Part 2):199-212.

[23] McLean R.L. 1961. General discussion. Am Rev Respir Dis 83:36-8.

[24] HHS. 2005. Pandemic Flu Plan, Supplement 7. U.S. Department of Health and Human Services. Last accessed February 20, 2006: http://www.hhs.gov/pandemicflu/plan/sup7.html..

[25] MMWR. 2006. Influenza vaccination of health care personnel. Last accessed March 21, 2006: http://www.cdc.gov/mmwr/preview/mmwrhtml/rr5502a1.htm.

[26] Wilde, J.A., et al. 1999. Effectiveness of Influenza Vaccine in Health Care Professionals. JAMA March 10, 1999 – Vol 281, No. 10.

[27] Salgado C.D., et al. 2004. Preventing Nosocomial Influenza Infection by Improving the Vaccine Acceptance Rate of Clinicians. Infection Control and Hospital Epidemiology. 2004 Nov: 25(11):923-8.

[28] HHS. 2005. Pandemic Influenza Plan, Appendix D. U.S. Department of Health and Human Services. Last accessed March 21, 2006: http://www.hhs.gov/pandemicflu/plan/appendixd.html.

[29] HHS. 2005. Pandemic Influenza Plan, Supplement 6. U.S. Department of Health and Human Services. Last accessed March 21, 2006: http://www.hhs.gov/pandemicflu/plan/sup6.html.

Infection Control

A successful infection control program for pandemic influenza utilizes the same strategies implemented for any infectious agent, including facility and environmental controls (i.e., engineering controls), standard operating procedures (i.e., administrative controls), personal protective clothing and equipment, and safe work practices. These strategies form the basis of standard precautions and transmission-based precautions. Given that the exact transmission pattern or patterns will not be known until after the pandemic influenza virus emerges, transmission-based infection control strategies may have to be modified to include additional selections of engineering controls, personal protective equipment (PPE), administrative controls, and/or safe work practices.

The infection control section of this document includes information about standard precautions and transmission-based precautions as they relate to the protection of healthcare workers.

Standard Precautions and Transmission-Based Precautions

Standard precautions are designed for the care of all patients, regardless of their diagnosis or presumed infection status. Transmission-based precautions are used for patients known or suspected to be infected or colonized with epidemiologically important pathogens that can be transmitted by airborne, droplet, or contact transmission. Some infectious agents require the application of several types of precautions to prevent transmission. For example, HHS/CDC recommends that standard, contact, and airborne precautions be implemented when caring for patients with varicella infection.[1, 2] Initially designed for the hospital setting, standard precautions and transmission-based precautions can be applied to a variety of healthcare settings, including the outpatient environment, the pre-hospital setting, and alternate care sites.

The infectious characteristics of pandemic influenza will not be known until after it emerges. Consequently, infection control plans will have to be adapted to the current knowledge of transmission and updated as new information becomes available. The Department of Health and Human Services (HHS) and its partners will provide updated epidemiologic information and infection control guidance at www.pandemicflu.gov. For a more complete discussion of standard precautions and transmission-based precautions, visit the HHS/CDC

Guideline for Isolation Precautions in Hospitals website at http://www.cdc.gov/ncidod/dhqp/gl_isolation.html.

Standard Precautions

Standard precautions should be used for all patients receiving care, regardless of their diagnosis or presumed infection status. Standard precautions apply to (1) blood; (2) all body fluids, secretions, and excretions except sweat, regardless of whether or not they contain visible blood; (3) nonintact skin; and (4) mucous membranes. Standard precautions are designed to reduce the risk of transmission of microorganisms from both recognized and unrecognized sources of infection in healthcare settings.

A risk assessment to determine necessary PPE and work practices to avoid contact with blood, body fluids, excretions, and secretions will help to customize standard precautions to the healthcare setting of interest. Standard precautions include:

- The use of gloves and facial (nose, mouth, and eye) protection by healthcare workers when providing care to coughing/sneezing patients.
- Hand hygiene before and after patient contact, and after removing gloves or other PPE. Routine hand hygiene is performed either by using an alcohol-based hand rub (preferably) or by washing hands with soap and water and using a single-use towel for drying hands. If hands are visibly dirty or soiled with blood or other body fluids, or if broken skin might have been exposed to infectious material, healthcare workers should wash their hands thoroughly with soap and water.
- Standard operating procedures to handle and disinfect patient care equipment, patient rooms, and soiled linen; prevent needlestick/sharp injuries; and address environmental cleaning, spills-management, and handling of waste.

Poor compliance with standard precautions among healthcare workers has been well described in the scientific literature.[3] Additionally, it has not been the routine practice of healthcare workers in many healthcare facilities to wear facial protection or to encourage respiratory hygiene among patients.

Implementation and enforcement of all standard precautions, including appropriate use of facial (eyes, nose, and mouth) protection when caring for respiratory patients, should be prioritized in all healthcare facilities in order to mitigate pandemic influenza transmission.

Contact Precautions

In addition to standard precautions, contact precautions are indicated for patients known or suspected to have serious illnesses easily transmitted by direct patient contact or by contact with items in the patient's environment. In addition to standard precautions, contact precautions include:

- Putting on PPE (such as gowns) prior to entry into a patient room and taking off PPE prior to exit.
- Dedicating patient care equipment.
- Limiting patient movement.
- Placing the patient in a private room or with patients who have active infection with the same microorganism or who are suspected to have active infection with the same microorganism but with no other infection (cohorting).

Some studies have shown contact transmission of human influenza. However, the importance of this transmission route remains unknown. Contact precautions are necessary during aerosol-generating procedures or when contact with infectious fluids is anticipated. Whether full contact precautions are indicated depends on the transmission pattern of the emerging pandemic influenza strain. If the pandemic virus is associated with diarrhea, contact precautions should be added.[4]

Droplet Precautions

Droplet precautions are indicated for patients known or suspected to have serious illnesses transmitted by large particle droplets, such as seasonal influenza, invasive *Haemophilus influenzae* type b disease and invasive *Neisseria meningitidis*. In addition to standard precautions, droplet precautions include the use of a surgical mask when working within 3 feet of the patient and the placement of the patient in a private room or with patients who have an active infection with the same microorganism but with no other infection (cohorting).

Although human seasonal influenza virus is transmitted primarily by contact with infectious droplets, some degree of airborne transmission occurs. Additionally, droplet precautions do not protect healthcare workers from infections resulting from aerosol transmission or during patient care activities that are likely to generate infectious aerosols, such as sputum induction or bronchoscopy.

Airborne Precautions

Airborne Precautions are designed to reduce the risk of airborne transmission of infectious agents. In addition to standard precautions, airborne precautions are used for patients known or suspected to have serious illnesses. Current clinical guidelines recommend that airborne precautions be used for such illnesses as H5N1 avian influenza, severe acute respiratory syndrome (SARS), measles, varicella, and tuberculosis.[1,5,6]

Airborne precautions include:

- Place patient in a negative pressure room (airborne infection isolation room) or area, if available.
- If a negative pressure room is not available or cannot be created with mechanical manipulation of the air, place patient in a single room.
- If a single room is not available, patients may be cohorted in designated multi-bed rooms or wards.
- Doors to any room or area housing patients must be kept closed when not being used for entry or egress.
- When possible, isolation rooms should have their own handwashing sink, toilet, and bath facilities.
- The number of persons entering the isolation room should be limited to the minimum number necessary for patient care and support.
- HHS/CDC recommends the use of a particulate respirator that is at least as protective as a National Institute for Occupational Safety and Health (NIOSH)-certified N95.[1,2] For a more complete discussion of respirator use during an influenza pandemic, see the section Respiratory Protection for Pandemic Influenza on page 27.

Airborne precautions against a respiratory illness should be implemented, as availability permits, when the circulating pathogen is known to cause severe disease, and the transmission characteristics of the infecting organism are not well characterized.

For patients for whom influenza is suspected or diagnosed, surveillance, vaccination, antiviral agents, and use of private rooms as much as feasible is recommended.[7] In contrast to tuberculosis, measles, and varicella, the pattern of disease spread for seasonal influenza does not suggest transmission across long distances (e.g., through ventilation systems); therefore, negative pressure rooms are not needed for patients with seasonal influenza.[8] Many hospitals encounter logistic difficulties and physical limitations when admitting multiple patients with suspected influenza during community outbreaks. If sufficient private rooms are unavailable, consider cohorting patients or, at the very least, avoid room-sharing with high-risk patients. For additional information regarding the airborne infection isolation rooms, see the section Airborne Infection Isolation Rooms on page 19.

Compliance with Infection Control

Healthcare administrators should emphasize those aspects of infection control already identified as "weak links" in the chain of infectious precautions—adherence to hand hygiene, consistent and proper use of PPE, and influenza vaccination of healthcare workers. The following section describes factors influencing compliance with infection control measures. Healthcare employers and employees should work together address these factors and enhance compliance with infection control recommendations.

Hand Hygiene Compliance

Although handwashing is well-known as a critical factor for infection control, low rates of healthcare worker compliance have been well documented. The HHS/CDC Healthcare Infection Control Practices Advisory Committee (HIC-PAC), in collaboration with the Society for Healthcare Epidemiology of America (SHEA), the Association for Professionals in Infection Control and Epidemiology (APIC), and the Infectious Diseases Society of America (IDSA) reviewed 33 studies from 1981 to 2000. They concluded that adherence of healthcare workers to recommended hand hygiene procedures has been poor, with mean baseline rates of 5 - 81 percent and an overall average of 40 percent.[3]

Several factors influence adherence to hand hygiene practices, including

- Being a physician or a nursing assistant, rather than a nurse
- Wearing gowns/gloves
- Understaffing and overcrowding
- Handwashing agents that cause irritation and dryness
- Lack of knowledge of guidelines
- Perceived lack of institutional priority for hand hygiene

It is important to recognize that healthcare workers report compliance with hand hygiene recommendations despite observations to the contrary. Recognition of the factors that influence compli-

---

Key Messages

Recognition of the factors that influence compliance with with infection control practices is important in order to enable healthcare employers to prioritize and customize compliance strategies.

Compliance strategies may include staff education, reminders in the workplace and routine observation and feedback.

Healthcare employers and employees should work together to develop an institutional safety climate that encourages compliance with recommended infection control practices.

---

ance to hand hygiene practices is important in order to enable healthcare employers to prioritize and customize compliance strategies. These strategies should be implemented to promote hand hygiene and may include staff education, reminders in the workplace and routine observation and feedback.

Appendix B contains extended information regarding risk factors for non-compliance with hand hygiene recommendations and strategies for successful promotion of hand hygiene. For a more complete discussion of the recommendations for hand hygiene and the scientific evidence, see the HHS/CDC *Guideline for Hand Hygiene in Healthcare Settings* at http://www.cdc.gov/hand-hygiene/.

Respiratory Protection Compliance

Studies have shown that healthcare worker compliance rates with respiratory protection are highly variable.[9, 10]

Healthcare workers fail to wear respirators for a number of reasons, and it is important to understand the nature of this resistance in order to overcome it. The following are the most frequently cited reasons for not wearing respirators:[11]

1. They are hot and uncomfortable.
2. They produce "pain spots" if poorly fitted.
3. They interfere with communication and performance.
4. They are not easily accessible when you need them.
5. They put the burden of safety on the wearer rather than the company.
6. They make the wearer look "funny," alarmist, not macho, or unattractive.
7. They produce labored breathing, increased heart rate, and perspiration.
8. They impair vision and can actually be a safety hazard.
9. They produce feelings of claustrophobia and anxiety.

The National Institute for Occupational Safety and Health (NIOSH) has published a guide that provides guidance on developing and implementing a respiratory protection program in the healthcare setting, TB Respiratory Protection Program in Health Care Facilities, September 1999, accessible at http://www.cdc.gov/niosh/99-143.html. Initially intended for protection against tuberculosis, the guidance can be adapted to address a variety of infectious pathogens, including pandemic influenza.

Healthcare employers should work hard to overcome employee resistance to wearing respirators and promote full compliance with the respiratory protection program. Strategies should be implemented to promote respirator use, such as staff education, reminders in the workplace and routine observation and feedback.

Organizational Factors that Affect Adherence to Infection Control

Lessons from the SARS outbreak showed that the most important factors affecting healthcare worker perceptions of risk and adherence to infection control practices were healthcare workers' perception that their facilities had clear policies and protocols, having adequate training in infection control procedures, and having specialists available.[12]

In a study among 1,716 hospital-based healthcare workers, Gershon et al. (1995) found that employees who perceived a strong commitment to safety at their workplace were over 2.5 times more likely to comply with universal precautions.[13] Another study of nurses found that the perception of PPE interference with work was the strongest predictor of failure to comply with universal precautions.[14] The same researchers examined the relative importance of safety climate, the availability of PPE, and individual employee characteristics as determinants of compliance with universal precautions. Safety climate was found to have the greatest association with proper infection control behaviors.[15]

Gershon et al. (2000) developed a safety climate scale (46 questions) to measure six different areas of a hospital safety climate:

- Senior management support for safety programs
- Absence of workplace barriers to safe work practices
- Cleanliness and orderliness of the worksite
- Minimal conflict and good communications among staff
- Frequent safety-related feedback and training by supervisors
- Availability of PPE and engineering controls[16]

This scale is available in the original reference and may be useful to assess problem areas of an institutional safety climate and increase adherence to infection control practices. Healthcare employers and employees should work together to develop an institutional safety climate that encourages compliance with recommended infection control practices.

Facility Design, Engineering, and Environmental Controls

Engineering controls are the preferred method to reduce transmission of infectious aerosols in areas used to house or evaluate patients with respiratory illness. The appropriate use of engineering controls and other control efforts will require frequent analysis of pandemic influenza transmission patterns in designated wards, in the facility, and in the community.

Existing healthcare facility layouts should be evaluated for potential enhancements of infection control. A SARS investigation in Ontario[17] noted that hospitals designed with open, public spaces encountered logistical difficulties and great expense in their efforts to control entry and, therefore, to control introduction of infectious diseases. Hospitals had an inadequate number of isolation rooms and negative pressure rooms. Triage areas were designed to streamline patient flow and enhance patient satisfaction, rather than to prioritize infection isolation or healthcare worker protection.

A desirable emergency room design includes a triage area that can be closed off as an isolation area, in the event of inadvertent contamination. Isolation areas should have adjacent rooms for staff

> ### Key Messages
>
> An influenza pandemic will increase the demand for hospital inpatient and intensive care unit beds and assisted ventilation services.
>
> Infectious disease and disaster management experts have predicted the need to use schools, stadiums, and other converted settings in the event of a pandemic that results in severe disease.
>
> The *National Strategy for Pandemic Influenza* calls for communities to anticipate large-scale augmentation of existing healthcare facilities.
>
> Limit admission of influenza patients to those with severe complications of influenza who cannot be cared for outside the hospital setting.
>
> Admit patients to either a single-patient room or an area designated for cohorting of patients with influenza.
>
> If possible, and when practical, use of an airborne isolation room may be considered when conducting aerosol-generating procedures.

to put on and take off scrubs, and to take showers. Facility planning should include storage space for augmented infection control items, including durable goods such as ventilators, portable high-efficiency particulate air (HEPA) filtration units, portable x-ray units, and respirators.

Thoughtful facility design includes rest and recuperation sites for responders. These sites can be stocked with healthy snacks and relaxation materials (e.g., music and movies), as well as pamphlets or notices about workforce support services.

Facility Capacity

An influenza pandemic may increase the demand for hospital inpatient and intensive care unit beds and assisted ventilation services by more than 25 percent.[18] Toronto clinicians reported that the intensive care unit capacity was a key factor that determined the number of SARS patients that could be managed. It was determined that approximately 20 percent of SARS patients required intensive care; therefore, a maximum number of SARS patients per facility could be calculated.[19]

HHS/CDC provided instructions that allow public health officials to estimate the demand for hospital resources and to estimate the number of deaths, both for a 1968-type of influenza pandemic and for a 1918-type of pandemic.[20] FluAid 2.0 and FluSurge 2.0 software estimate the number of deaths, hospitalizations, outpatient visits, and the increased demand for hospital resources (e.g., beds, intensive care, or ventilators for both scenarios). For additional information see Appendix A.

Alternate care sites may be developed at federal or state discretion to ease the burden of care on healthcare facilities. For additional information regarding alternate care sites, see section Alternate Care Sites on page 47.

Engineering Controls in Improvised Settings

Infectious disease and disaster management experts have predicted the need to use schools, stadiums, and other converted settings in the event of a pandemic that results in severe disease. The *National Strategy for Pandemic Influenza*[21] calls for communities to anticipate large-scale augmentation of existing healthcare facilities.

During the SARS outbreak of 2004, the North York General Hospital in Toronto converted two nearly constructed hospital wings into SARS wards. Additionally, a tent clinic was built on an ambulance loading dock to triage the general public presenting with possible SARS. A more detailed description of the converted healthcare settings,

including the implementation of engineering of controls, is available in Loutfy et al. 2004.[19]

Airborne Infection Isolation Rooms

Although the need to isolate patients with highly pathogenic infections is a central tenet of infection control, a large percentage of U.S. hospitals have no isolation rooms. Only 61.7 percent of hospitals responding to the American Hospital Association 2004 annual survey reported having an airborne infection isolation room.[22]

Airborne infection isolation rooms receive numerous air changes per hour (ACH) (>12 ACH for new construction as of 2001; >6 ACH for construction before 2001), and is under negative pressure, such that the direction of the air flow is from the outside adjacent space (e.g., the corridor) into the room. The air in an airborne infection isolation room is preferably exhausted to the outside, but may be recirculated provided that the return air is filtered through a high-efficiency particulate air (HEPA) filter.

For more information, consult the HHS/CDC *Guidelines for Environmental Infection Control in Health Care Facilities*, available at http://www.cdc.gov/ncidod/dhqp/gl_environinfection.html.

For care of pandemic influenza patients in the hospital:[4]

- Limit admission of influenza patients to those with severe complications of influenza who cannot be cared for outside the hospital setting.
- Admit patients to either a single-patient room or an area designated for cohorting of patients with influenza.
- If possible, and when practical, use of an airborne isolation room may be considered when conducting aerosol-generating procedures.

Engineering Controls for Aerosol-Generating Procedures for Patients with Pandemic Influenza

If possible, and when practical, use of an airborne isolation room may be considered when conducting aerosol-generating procedures,[4,6] such as the following:

- Endotracheal intubation
- Aerosolized or nebulized medication administration
- Diagnostic sputum induction/collection
- Bronchoscopy
- Airway suctioning
- Positive pressure ventilation *via* face mask

(e.g., BiPAP and CPAP)
- High-frequency oscillatory ventilation

If a negative pressure room is not available, the following strategies may be considered. However, there is only limited scientific evidence to support these strategies:[6, 23, 24]

- Perform the procedure in a private room, separated from other patients.
- If possible, increase air changes, increase negative pressure relative to the hallway, and avoid recirculation of the room air.
- If recirculation of the air is unavoidable, pass the air through a HEPA filter before recirculation.
- Keep doors closed except when entering or leaving the room, and minimize entry to and exit from the room.

Cohorting

If single rooms are not available, patients infected with the same organisms can be cohorted (share rooms). These rooms should be in a well-defined area that is clearly separated from other patient care areas used for uninfected patients.

During a pandemic, other respiratory viruses (e.g., non-pandemic influenza, respiratory syncytial virus, parainfluenza virus) may be circulating concurrently in a community. Therefore, to prevent cross-transmission of respiratory viruses, whenever possible assign only patients with confirmed pandemic influenza to the same room. Management of cohort areas should incorporate the following:[4]

- Designated areas should be used for cohorting pandemic influenza-infected patients. At the height of a pandemic, laboratory testing to confirm pandemic influenza is likely to be limited, in which case cohorting should be based on having symptoms consistent with pandemic influenza. Suspected cases of pandemic influenza should be housed separately from confirmed cases of pandemic influenza.
- Whenever possible, healthcare workers assigned to cohorted patient care units should be experienced healthcare workers and should not "float" or be assigned to other patient care areas.
- The number of persons entering the cohorted area should be limited to the minimum number necessary for patient care and support.
- Limit patient transport by having portable x-ray equipment available in cohort areas, if possible.
- Healthcare workers assigned to cohorted

patient care units should be aware that pandemic influenza-infected patients may be concurrently infected or colonized with other pathogenic organisms (e.g., *Staphylococcus aureus and Clostridium difficile*) and should use standard and applicable transmission-based infection control precautions to prevent transmission of healthcare-associated infections.

Engineering Controls in Diagnostic and Research Laboratories

During the Pandemic Alert Period, specimens from suspected cases of human infection with novel influenza viruses should be sent for testing to public health laboratories with proper biocontainment facilities. For example, reverse transcriptase polymerase chain reaction (RT-PCR) can be done in a Biosafety Level 2 laboratory but highly pathogenic avian influenza and highly pathogenic pandemic influenza virus isolation should be conducted in a Biosafety Level 3 laboratory with enhancements or higher as dictated by an appropriate risk assessment.

Additional information on laboratory biocontainment is provided in the HHS publication *Biosafety in Microbiological and Biomedical Laboratories*.[25] Pneumatic tube systems are not advisable to transport specimens that may contain a highly pathogenic, live virus. Guidelines on when to send specimens or isolates of suspected novel avian or human strains to HHS/CDC for reference testing are available in Appendix 3 of the HHS *Pandemic Influenza Plan* at http://www.hhs.gov/pandemicflu/plan/sup2.html#app3.[26] The American Society for Microbiology maintains a list of emergency contacts in state public health laboratories.[27]

Autopsy Rooms for Cases of Pandemic Influenza

Safety procedures for pandemic influenza-infected human bodies should be consistent with those used for any autopsy procedure with potentially infected remains. In general, the hazards of working in the autopsy room seem to depend more on contact with infected material, particularly with splashes on body surfaces, than to inhalation of infectious material. However, if the pandemic influenza-infected patient died during the infectious period, the lungs may still contain virus and additional respiratory protection is needed during procedures performed on the lungs or during procedures that generate small-particle aerosols (e.g., use of power saws and washing intestines).

Protective autopsy settings for pandemic influenza-infected humans include the use of an airborne infection isolation room (see the section Airborne Infection Isolation Rooms on page 19). Exhaust systems around the autopsy table should direct air (and aerosols) away from healthcare workers performing the procedure (e.g., exhaust downward). It is important to use containment devices whenever possible (e.g., biosafety cabinets for the handling of smaller specimens). Therefore, an examiner conducting postmortem exams of pandemic influenza-infected patients will use airborne precautions, including a particulate respirator, as is recommended for postmortem exams of avian influenza-infected patients and SARS-infected patients.[28]

Administrative Controls

Respiratory Hygiene/Cough Etiquette

Respiratory hygiene/cough etiquette, procedures should be used for all patients with respiratory symptoms (e.g., coughing and sneezing). The impact of covering coughs and sneezes and placing a mask on a coughing/sneezing patient on the containment of respiratory droplets and secretions or on the transmission of respiratory infections has not been quantified. However, any measure that limits the dispersion of respiratory droplets should reduce the opportunity for transmission. Masking some patients may be difficult, in which case the emphasis should be on cough etiquette. The elements of cough etiquette are listed below.

For additional information, see *Respiratory Hygiene/Cough Etiquette in Healthcare Settings* at http://www.cdc.gov/flu/professionals/infection control/resphygiene.htm.

Pandemic Influenza Specimen Collection and Transport

All human specimens of secretions and excretions should be regarded as potentially infectious. Healthcare workers who collect or transport clinical specimens should consistently adhere to recommended infection control precautions to minimize their exposure. Potentially infectious specimens should be placed in leakproof specimen bags for transport, labeled or color coded for transport and handled by personnel who are familiar with safe handling practices and spill clean-up procedures. Healthcare workers who collect specimens from pandemic-infected patients should also wear PPE as described for employees performing direct patient care.

Respiratory Hygiene/Cough Etiquette

Educate persons with respiratory illness and coughing or sneezing to:

- Cover their mouths and noses with a tissue and dispose of used tissues in no-touch waste containers.
- Use a mask when tolerated, especially during periods of increased respiratory infection activity in the community.
- Perform hand hygiene after contact with respiratory secretions and contaminated objects or materials (e.g., handwashing with soap and water, alcohol-based hand rub, or antiseptic handwash).
- Stand or sit at least 3 feet from other persons, if possible.

Healthcare facilities should promote respiratory hygiene by:

- Posting signs requesting that patients and family members immediately report symptoms of respiratory illness on arrival to the facility and use cough etiquette.
- Posting signs requesting that persons with respiratory illness refrain from visiting the healthcare facility if they are not seeking medical treatment.
- Providing conveniently located masks, tissues, and alcohol-based hand rubs for waiting areas and patient evaluation areas to facilitate source control.
- Providing no-touch receptacles for used tissue disposal.
- Ensuring that supplies for handwashing (i.e., soap, disposable towels) are consistently available where sinks are located.
- Educating healthcare workers, patients, family members, and visitors on the importance of containing respiratory droplets and secretions to help prevent transmission of influenza and other infections.

Specimens should be hand delivered where possible. Pneumatic tube systems are not advisable to transport specimens that may contain a highly pathogenic, live virus. For additional information about specimen collection, visit WHO's website at http://www.who.int/csr/disease/avian_influenza/guidelines/humanspecimens/en/index.html.

Patient Transport within Healthcare Facilities

Influenza-infected patients' respiratory secretions are the principle source of infectious material in healthcare settings. Maintaining source control of patient secretions will limit the opportunities for nosocomial (in hospital) transmission. The following methods of source control are consistent with those recommended for other serious respiratory infections (e.g., SARS, avian influenza, and tuberculosis).[4, 28,29]

- Surgical and procedure masks are appropriate for use by pandemic influenza-infected patients to contain respiratory droplets and should be worn by suspected or confirmed pandemic influenza-infected patients during transport or when care is necessary outside of the isolation room/area.
- Limit the movement and transport of patients from the isolation room/area for essential purposes only. Inform the receiving area/facility as soon as possible, prior to the patient's arrival, of the patient's diagnosis and of the precautions that are indicated. Use mobile diagnostic services (e.g., mobile X-ray and CT scan) when available.
- If transport outside the isolation room/area is required, the patient should wear a surgical mask and perform hand hygiene after contact with respiratory secretions.
- If the patient cannot tolerate a mask (e.g., due to the patient's age or deteriorating respiratory status), instruct the patient (or parent of pediatric patient) to cover the nose and mouth with a tissue during coughing and sneezing, or use the most practical alternative to contain respiratory secretions. If possible, instruct the patient to perform hand hygiene after respiratory hygiene.
- Identify appropriate paths, separated from main traffic routes as much as possible, for entry and movement of pandemic influenza patients in the facility, and determine how these pathways will be controlled (e.g., dedicated pandemic influenza corridors and elevators).
- If there is patient contact with surfaces, these surfaces should be cleaned and disinfected.
- Healthcare workers transporting unmasked patients with suspected or confirmed pandemic influenza-infected patients should wear an N95 or higher NIOSH-certified respirator.

Pre-Hospital Care and Patient Transport Outside Healthcare Facilities

During an influenza pandemic, patients will still require emergency transport to a healthcare facility. The recommendations in the table on page 23 are designed to protect healthcare workers, including emergency medical services personnel, during pre-hospital care and transport. These recommendations can be instituted when patients are identified as having symptoms consistent with an influenza-like illness or routinely, regardless of symptoms, when pandemic influenza is in the community.

Staff Education and Training

It is incumbent upon healthcare employers to educate employees about the hazards to which they are exposed and to provide reasonable means by which to abate those hazards. The independent SARS Commission established by the government of Ontario noted that many healthcare staff were not adequately trained in protecting themselves against infectious agents. The Commission noted deficiencies in safety training and the proper use of personal protective equipment.[30]

Effective staff training is consistent with facility policies and reinforces infection control strategies. Support from the healthcare institution at the top management and supervisory levels is essential for a successful program. Examples of educational goals and objectives for pandemic infection control strategies include:

- Educate healthcare workers about recommended infection control precautions for suspected or confirmed pandemic influenza-infected patients. At a minimum, healthcare workers should follow contact and droplet precautions for all patients with acute respiratory illness.
- Ensure that clinicians know where and how to promptly report a pandemic influenza case to hospital and public health officials.
- Communicate planning strategies that address when confirmed pandemic influenza-infected patients have been admitted to the facility, nosocomial surveillance should be heightened for evidence of transmission to other patients and staff.
- Educate healthcare workers and visitors on the correct use of PPE and hand hygiene.
  - Recommended steps for placement and removal of PPE and performance of hand hygiene.
  - Appropriate procedures to select a particulate respirator that fits well.

(continued on page 24)

	Screen all patients for influenza-like illness.* If influenza is suspected, implement the following strategies:	Without relying on patient screening, routinely implement the following strategies:
Engineering Controls	• Optimize the vehicle's ventilation to increase the volume of air exchange during transport. The vehicle's ventilation system should be operated in the non-recirculating mode and should bring in as much outdoor air as possible. • When possible, use vehicles that have separate driver and patient compartments that can provide separate ventilation to each area. In this situation, drivers do not require particulate respirators.	• Optimize the vehicle's ventilation to increase the volume of air exchange during transport. The vehicle's ventilation system should be operated in the non-recirculating mode and should bring in as much outdoor air as possible. • When possible, use vehicles that have separate driver and patient compartments that can provide separate ventilation to each area. In this situation, drivers do not require particulate respirators.
Administrative Controls	• Educate healthcare workers engaged in medical transport about the risks of aerosol-generating procedures. • Notify the receiving facility as soon as possible, prior to arrival, that a patient with suspected pandemic influenza infection is being transported to the facility and of the precautions that are indicated. • Minimize the opportunity for contamination of supplies and equipment inside the vehicle (e.g., ensure that all cabinetry remains closed during transport). • Continue to follow standard infection control procedures, such as standard precautions, recommended procedures for waste disposal and standard practices for disinfection of the emergency vehicle and patient care equipment.	• Educate healthcare workers engaged in medical transport about the risks of aerosol-generating procedures. • Notify the receiving facility as soon as possible, prior to arrival, that a patient with suspected pandemic influenza infection is being transported to the facility and of the precautions that are indicated. • Minimize the opportunity for contamination of supplies and equipment inside the vehicle (e.g., ensure that all cabinetry remains closed during transport). • Continue to follow standard infection control procedures, such as standard precautions, recommended procedures for waste disposal and standard practices for disinfection of the emergency vehicle and patient care equipment.
Personal Protective Equipment	• If tolerated by the patients, place a surgical mask on all patients with respiratory illness to contain droplets expelled during coughing. If this is not possible (i.e., would further compromise respiratory status, or is difficult for the patient to wear), have the patient cover the mouth and nose with a tissue when coughing, or use the most practical alternative to contain respiratory secretions. • Healthcare workers transporting patients with influenza-like illness should use a respirator (N95 or higher). If respirators are not available, healthcare workers should wear a surgical mask.	• Consider routine use of surgical or procedure masks for all patients during transport when pandemic influenza is in the community. • Healthcare workers transporting patients should use a respirator (N95 or higher). If respirators are not available, healthcare workers should wear a surgical mask.

*The Sentinel Provider Network definition of influenza-like illness is fever (>100°F or 37.8°C) and sore throat and/or cough in the absence of a known cause other than influenza.

- Train persons who will be likely to use particulate respirators on how to put them on and how to perform user seal checks.
- Provide respiratory etiquette educational materials and supplies to coughing individuals.
- Train infection control monitors to observe and correct deficiencies in healthcare worker and visitor adherence to proper hygiene and PPE use.
- Use simulations (i.e., "table top" or other exercises) to test the facility's response capacities. The exercise should be realistic and should continue until limiting factors and deficiencies are identified.
- Develop risk communication materials for healthcare workers, patients, and patient families/visitors.

Staff education and training should be available in formats accessible to individuals with disabilities and/or limited English proficiency; and should also target the educational level of the intended audience.

Care of the Deceased

Follow standard facility practices for care of the deceased. Practices should include standard precautions for contact with blood and body fluids. For more information regarding care of deceased, see *Avian Influenza, Including Influenza A (H5N1), in Humans: WHO Interim Infection Control Guideline For Health Care Facilities*, April 24, 2006, available at: http://www.who.int/csr/disease/avian_influenza/guidelines/infectioncontrol1/en/.

Patient Discharge

If the patient is discharged while possibly still infectious, family members should be educated on hand hygiene, cough etiquette, the use of a surgical or procedure mask by a patient who is still coughing and any additional infection control measures identified in forthcoming guidance or recommendations. Updated guidance and recommendations will be posted on www.pandemicflu.gov whenever they become available.

Visitor Policies

Visitors should be strictly limited to those necessary for the patient's well-being and care, and should be advised about the possible risk of acquiring infection. Care of patients in isolation becomes a challenge when there are inadequate resources, or when the patient has poor hygienic habits, deliberately contaminates the environment, or cannot be expected to assist in maintaining infection control

precautions to limit transmission of microorganisms (e.g., children, patients with an altered mental state, or elderly persons). Such patients should be managed on a case-by-case basis, balancing the rights of the patient with the risk they may present to others.

- Visitors should be provided PPE to comply with recommended precautions and should be instructed on how to properly put on, take off, and dispose of PPE. They should also be instructed on proper hand hygiene practices prior to entry to the patient isolation room/area.
- Communication of policies and procedures to visitors should be available in formats accessible to individuals with disabilities and/or limited English proficiency; and should also target the educational level of the intended audience.
- Legal guardians of pediatric patients should be allowed, when possible, to accompany the patient throughout the hospitalization.
- Parents/relatives/legal guardians may assist in providing care to pandemic influenza-infected patients in special situations (e.g., lack of resources, pediatric patients, etc.) if adequate training and supervision of PPE use and hand hygiene is ensured.
- Because family members may have been exposed to pandemic influenza via the patient or similar environmental exposures, all family members and visitors should be screened for symptoms of respiratory illness upon entry to the facility.
- Symptomatic family members or visitors should be considered possible pandemic influenza cases and should be evaluated for pandemic influenza infection.

Healthcare Worker Vaccination

An influenza pandemic occurs when a new version of an influenza virus develops the capability to infect humans and to spread easily and rapidly between people. Sometimes such new virus versions come from influenza viruses that previously affected only birds or animals, but which have mutated and thus have developed the capabilities to infect humans and spread easily among humans.

It is believed that humans will initially have little, if any, immunity to a pandemic influenza virus and, therefore, that everyone will be susceptible to infection. The HHS *Pandemic Influenza Plan* assumes that one in five working adults will experience clinical disease in a pandemic influenza outbreak.[18] It also presumes that, in an affected community, a pandemic outbreak will last about 6 to 8 weeks with at least two pandemic disease waves likely to occur.

Influenza vaccination is the most effective method currently available to prevent people from getting infected. During outbreaks of seasonal influenza, vaccination against that season's influenza subtypes usually prevents infection. If infection is not fully prevented, a vaccination may lessen the severity of the resulting illness.

Once a new type of influenza virus emerges, it usually takes four to six months to produce a vaccine for that virus, using currently available vaccine production methods. There may be limited or no pandemic influenza vaccine available for administration to individuals in the first six months or longer during a pandemic. However, HHS plans to work with the pharmaceutical industry to produce and stockpile up to 20 million courses of vaccine against each circulating influenza virus with pandemic potential during the pre-pandemic period.[31] Stockpiled vaccine will be designated for personnel who perform critical and essential functions. Medical and public health employees who are involved in direct patient contact and other support services essential for direct patient care are likely to be given high priority for receipt of stockpiled vaccine.[32]

Annual seasonal influenza immunization rates among healthcare workers in the United States remain low; coverage among healthcare workers in 2003 was 40.1 percent.[33] Therefore, to diminish absence due to illness, it is advisable for healthcare facilities to encourage and/or provide seasonal influenza vaccination for their staff, including volunteers, yearly, during the months of October and November.

Vaccination strategy recommendations for healthcare facilities in preparation for or in response to a pandemic influenza outbreak include:[34]

- Promote annual seasonal influenza vaccination among staff and volunteers.
- Communicate with state and local health departments as to the availability of stockpiles of vaccine for the specific pandemic influenza subtype and follow federal and local recommendations for administering the vaccine to healthcare workers.
- Plan for rapid vaccination of healthcare workers as recommended by federal agencies and state health departments, if vaccine for the pandemic influenza virus becomes available.
- Have a system for documentation of influenza

vaccination of healthcare workers, since vaccination for pandemic influenza may require two doses.

Antiviral Medication for Prophylaxis and Treatment in Healthcare Workers

The HHS *Pandemic Influenza Plan* assumes that oseltamivir will be the antiviral medication of choice in the event of an outbreak of pandemic influenza.[31] It assumes that supplies will be limited[31] and that the primary source of oseltamivir will be from federal stockpiles. Oseltamivir can be used to treat persons who are diagnosed with influenza; however, for optimal effectiveness, the treatment should be initiated within 48 hours of the onset of flu-like symptoms.

Oseltamivir may also be used prophylactically to decrease the chance of infection in persons, such as healthcare workers, who have had exposure to pandemic influenza patients. Information on the advisability of using other antiviral medications during an influenza pandemic will be determined and communicated after the susceptibility of the causative viral subtype has been studied.

Healthcare facilities should maintain contact with federal and local health departments concerning the availability of antiviral medications and the recommendations to administer antiviral medications as treatment or as prophylaxis to healthcare workers and emergency medical personnel who have direct patient contact.[34] Regardless of the availability of antiviral medication, it should not be used in lieu of a full infection control program.

- When considering antiviral prophylaxis, be sure to evaluate appropriate candidates for contraindications, answer their questions, review adverse effects, and explain the risks and benefits.
- Maintain a log of persons on antiviral medications, persons evaluated and not receiving prophylaxis, doses dispensed, and adverse effects.
- Periodically evaluate and update antiviral prophylaxis policies and procedures.

Occupational Medicine Services

Employee Protection
Transmission in healthcare facilities was a major factor in the spread of SARS during the 2003 global epidemic. Factors that likely contributed to the disproportionate rate of transmission in healthcare settings included (1) exposure to infectious droplets and aerosols via use of ventilators, nebulizers, endotracheal intubation, and other procedures and

(2) frequent and prolonged close contact of employees to patients, their secretions, and potentially contaminated environments.[35] Case recognition and implementation of appropriate precautions greatly reduced the risks of SARS transmission. However, even with appropriate precautions, there were isolated reports of transmission to healthcare workers in the settings of aerosol-producing procedures and lapses in infection control techniques.[29]

Healthcare workers are also members of the community, and during seasonal influenza outbreaks their infectious illnesses may or may not be related to workplace infectious exposures. Seasonal vaccines will not protect against pandemic influenza, but will help prevent concurrent infection with seasonal influenza and pandemic influenza, which will minimize the possibility of reassortment of the virus. Protective levels of antibodies are usually detectable 2 to 4 weeks after vaccination with seasonal influenza vaccine. In addition, healthcare workers who provide direct patient care may be exposed to pandemic influenza viruses. These employees should be monitored for illness and supported as needed.

Recommendations for Occupational Health Administrators

Protecting healthcare workers benefits both the community and the individual employee. Comprehensive occupational health programs can limit transmission from infected employees and allow them to continue working while their services are in extreme demand.

Surveillance Activities

- Keep a register of healthcare workers who have provided care for pandemic influenza-infected patients (confirmed or probable cases).
- Keep a register of healthcare workers who have recovered from pandemic influenza (confirmed or probable cases).
- Have a healthcare worker influenza-like illness surveillance system in the healthcare facility, including encouragement for self-reporting by symptomatic healthcare workers.
- Have a system to monitor work absenteeism for health reasons, especially in healthcare workers providing direct patient care.
- Screen all healthcare workers providing care to pandemic influenza-infected patients for influenza-like symptoms before each daily shift. Symptomatic healthcare workers should be evaluated and excluded from duty.

- Clinical employees believed to have had significant clinical exposure to a highly pathogenic influenza strain should be evaluated; counseled about the risk of transmission to others; and monitored for fever, respiratory symptoms, sore throat, rhinorrhea (runny nose), chills, rigors, myalgia, headache, and diarrhea.

Vaccination and Antivirals

- Vaccinate healthcare workers against seasonal influenza and monitor compliance.
- Coordinate with public health officials for local policy on antiviral prophylaxis of healthcare workers and assistance for obtaining adequate supplies of neuraminidase inhibitors for prophylaxis of healthcare workers providing care for pandemic influenza-infected patients.[28] Develop a system to provide neuraminidase inhibitors to healthcare workers exposed to pandemic influenza-infected patients according to local and national policies.

Occupational Medical Surveillance and Staffing Decisions

Occupational health played a major role in determining which healthcare workers should return to work during the SARS outbreaks.[19] In future outbreaks, individual risk assessment and fitness for duty determinations should be accomplished more efficiently with the support of updated staff medical records and with serologic testing results, if available.

- If possible, perform serologic and other testing for pandemic influenza on healthcare workers with influenza-like illness and who have had likely exposures to pandemic influenza-infected patients.
- Healthcare workers with serological evidence of pandemic influenza infection should have protective antibodies against this strain and can be prioritized for the care of pandemic influenza patients. These employees could also be prioritized to provide care for patients who are at risk for serious complications from influenza (e.g., transplant patients and neonates). However, be aware that subsequent "waves" of influenza infection may be caused by a different influenza strain.
- Some healthcare workers have an increased risk of complications due to pandemic influenza (e.g., pregnant women, immunocompromised persons and persons with respiratory diseases). Care should be taken to provide appropriate education, training and policies

that comply with federal, state and local laws to adequately protect these employees.

- Healthcare workers who are ill should not be involved in direct patient care since they may be more vulnerable to other infections and may be more likely to develop severe illness if infected with pandemic influenza. In addition, ill healthcare workers can transmit their illness to vulnerable patients.

Personal Protective Equipment

Gloves

HHS recommends the use of gloves made of latex, vinyl, nitrile, or other synthetic materials as appropriate, when there is contact with blood and other bodily fluids, including respiratory secretions.

- There is no need to double-glove.
- Gloves should be removed and discarded after patient care.
- Gloves should not be washed or reused.
- Hand hygiene should be done after glove removal.

Because glove supplies may be limited in the event of pandemic influenza, other barriers such as disposable paper towels should be used when there is limited contact with respiratory secretions, such as handling used facial tissues. Hand hygiene should be practiced consistently in this situation.[4]

Gowns[4]

- Healthcare workers should wear an isolation gown when it is anticipated that soiling of clothes or uniform with blood or other bodily fluids, including respiratory secretions, may occur. HHS states that most routine pandemic influenza patient encounters do not necessitate the use of gowns. Examples of when a gown may be needed include procedures such as intubation or when closely holding a pediatric patient.
- Isolation gowns can be disposable and made of synthetic material or reusable and made of washable cloth.
- Gowns should be the appropriate size to fully cover the areas requiring protection.
- After patient care is performed, the gown should be removed and placed in a laundry receptacle or waste container, as appropriate. Hand hygiene should follow.

Goggles/Face Shields

The HHS Pandemic Influenza Plan does not recommend the use of goggles or face shields for routine contact with patients with pandemic influenza; however, if sprays or splatters of infectious material are likely, it states that goggles or a face shield should be worn as recommended for standard precautions.[4] For additional information about eye protection for infection control, visit NIOSH's website at http://www.cdc.gov/niosh/topics/eye/eye-infectious.html.

If a pandemic influenza patient is coughing, any healthcare worker who needs to be within 3 feet of the infected patient is likely to encounter sprays of infectious material. Eye and face protection should be used in this situation, as well as during the performance of aerosol-generating procedures.

Respiratory Protection for Pandemic Influenza

While droplet transmission is likely to be the major route of exposure for pandemic influenza, as is the case with seasonal influenza, it may not be the only route. Given the potential severity of health consequences (illness and death) associated with pandemic influenza, a comprehensive pandemic influenza preparedness plan should also address airborne transmission to ensure that healthcare workers are protected against all potential routes of exposure. Establishment of a comprehensive respiratory protection program with all of the elements specified in OSHA's Respiratory Protection standard (29 CFR 1910.134) is needed to achieve the highest levels of protection. Additional information on the Respiratory Protection standard is included in Appendix C in this document. More information on the elements of a comprehensive respiratory protection program and the use of respirators can be found at http://www.osha.gov/SLTC/respiratoryprotection/index.html.

Healthcare workers are at risk of exposure to airborne infectious agents, including influenza. For some types of airborne infectious agents (such as SARS), healthcare workers are not only at risk for illness but may become a potential source of infection to patients and others. Selection of appropriate respiratory PPE requires an understanding of the airborne infectious agents, their infectious and aerodynamic properties, the operating characteristics of the PPE, and the behaviors and characteristics of the healthcare workers using the PPE. Many different types of respiratory PPE are available to protect healthcare workers, each with a different set of advantages and disadvantages.

There will continue to be uncertainty about the modes of transmission until the actual pandemic influenza strain emerges. It is expected that there will be a worldwide shortage of respirators if and when a pandemic occurs. Employers and employees should not count on obtaining any additional protective equipment not already purchased and stockpiled. Therefore, it is important for healthcare facilities to consider respiratory protection for essential personnel to assure that employees are ready, willing, and able to care for the general population.

Surgical Masks and Respirators

Although some disposable respirators look similar to surgical masks, it is important that healthcare workers understand the significant functional difference between disposable respirators and surgical masks.

- Respirators are designed to reduce an individual's exposure to airborne contaminants, such as particles, gases, or vapors. An air-purifying respirator accomplishes this by filtering the contaminant out of the air before it can be inhaled by the person wearing the respirator. A type of respirator commonly found in healthcare workplaces is the filtering facepiece particulate respirator (often referred to as an "N95"). It is designed to protect against particulate hazards. Since airborne biological agents such as bacteria or viruses are particles, they can be filtered by particulate respirators. To assure a consistent level of performance, the respirator's filtering efficiency is tested and certified by NIOSH.

- In comparison, surgical masks are not designed to prevent inhalation of airborne contaminants. Their ability to filter small particles varies greatly and cannot be assured to protect healthcare workers against airborne infectious agents. Instead, their underlying purpose is to prevent contamination of a sterile field or work environment by trapping bacteria and respiratory secretions that are expelled by the wearer (i.e., protecting the patient against infection from the healthcare worker). Surgical masks are also used as a physical barrier to protect the healthcare worker from hazards such as splashes of blood or bodily fluids. When both fluid protection (e.g., blood splashes) and respiratory protection are needed, a "surgical N95" respirator can be used. This respirator is approved by FDA and certified by NIOSH.

Another important difference in protecting healthcare workers from airborne infectious agents is the way respirators and surgical masks fit the user's face. Respirators are designed to provide a tight seal between the sealing surface of the respirator and the person's face. A proper seal between the user's face and the respirator forces inhaled air to be pulled through the respirator's filter material and not through gaps between the face and respirator. Surgical masks, however, are not designed to seal tightly against the user's face. During inhalation, potentially contaminated air can pass through gaps between the face and the surgical mask, thus avoiding being pulled through the material of the mask and losing any filtration that it may provide.

When personal protective equipment is necessary to protect against droplet transmission of infectious agents, employees must place a barrier between the source of the droplet (e.g., a sneeze) and their mucosal surfaces. Such protection could include a surgical mask to cover the mouth and nose and safety glasses to cover the eyes. Recent studies show that aerosol penetration through a surgical mask is highly dependent on particle size, mask construction, and breathing flow rate. One study showed that penetration rates for submicron particles could be as high as 80 percent for surgical masks.[36] Even relatively unconventional uses (e.g., the wearing of multiple surgical masks) have been shown to be less protective than NIOSH-certified respirators. For example, research has shown that the use of up to five surgical masks worn by volunteers results in particle reduction of only 63 percent for one mask, 74 percent for two masks, 78 percent for three masks, and 82 percent for five masks, compared with a recommended reduction of at least 95 percent for properly fitted N95 respirators.[37]

To help employers and employees better understand respirators, the following paragraphs discuss their construction, classification, and use.

Respirators

A respirator is a personal protective device that is worn on the face, covers at least the nose and mouth, and is used to reduce the wearer's risk of inhaling hazardous gases, vapors, or airborne particles (e.g., dust or droplet nuclei containing infectious agents). The many types of respirators available include:

- Particulate respirators that filter out airborne particles.
- "Gas masks" that filter out chemical gases and vapors.
- Airline respirators that use a hose/pipe to provide a flow of clean air from a remote source.
- Self-contained breathing apparatus that provide clean air from a compressed air tank worn by the user.

Particulate respirators can be divided into several types:

- Disposable or filtering facepiece respirators, where the entire respirator facepiece is comprised of filter material. It is discarded when it becomes unsuitable for further use due to excessive breathing resistance (e.g., particulate clogging the filter), unacceptable contamination/soiling, or physical damage.
- Reusable or elastomeric respirators, where the facepiece is cleaned, repaired, and reused, but the filter cartridges are discarded and replaced when they become unsuitable for further use.
- Powered air-purifying respirators, where a battery-powered blower pulls contaminated air through filters, then moves the filtered air to the wearer.

All respirators used by employees are required to be tested and certified by NIOSH. NIOSH uses very high standards to test and approve respirators for occupational uses. NIOSH-certified particulate respirators are marked with the manufacturer's name, the part number, the protection provided by the filter (e.g., N95), and "NIOSH." This information is printed on the facepiece, exhalation valve cover, or head straps. If a respirator does not have these markings and does not appear on one of the following lists, it has not been certified by NIOSH.

A list of all NIOSH-certified disposable respirators is available at http://www.cdc.gov/niosh/npptl/respirators/disp_part/particlist.html. NIOSH also maintains a database of all NIOSH-certified respirators regardless of respirator type (the Certified Equipment List), which can be accessed at http://www.cdc.gov/niosh/celintro.html.

Classifying Particulate Respirators and Particulate Filters

An N95 respirator is one of nine types of particulate respirators. Particulate respirators are also known as "air-purifying respirators" because they protect by filtering particles out of the air as you breathe. Particulate respirators protect only against particles—not gases or vapors. Since airborne biological agents such as bacteria or viruses are particles, they can be filtered by particulate respirators.

Respirator filters that remove at least 95 percent of airborne particles, during "worst case" testing using the "most-penetrating" size of particle, are given a 95 rating. Those that filter out at least 99 percent of the particles under the same conditions receive a 99 rating, and those that filter at least 99.97 percent (essentially 100 percent) receive a 100 rating.

In addition, filters in this family are given a designation of N, R, or P to convey their ability to function in the presence of oils.

"N" if they are Not resistant to oil.
"R" if they are somewhat Resistant to oil.
"P" if they are strongly resistant (i.e., oilProof).

This rating is important in work settings where oils may be present because some industrial oils can degrade the filter performance to the point that it does not filter adequately. (Note: This is generally not an issue in healthcare facilities.) Thus, the three filter efficiencies combined with the three oil designations leads to nine types of particulate respirator filter materials:

Particulate Respirator Filter Type	Percentage (%) of 0.3 μm airborne particles filtered out	Not resistant to oil	Somewhat resistant to oil	Strongly resistant to oil (oil-proof)
N95	95	X		
N99	99	X		
N100	99.97	X		
R95	95		X	
R99	99		X	
R100	99.97		X	
P95	95			X
P99	99			X
P100	99.97			X

Recent HHS/CDC infection control guidance documents provide recommendations that healthcare workers protect themselves from diseases potentially spread through the air by wearing a fit tested respirator at least as protective as a NIOSH-certified N95 respirator. Employees can wear any of the particulate respirators for protection against diseases spread through the air, if they are NIOSH-certified and if they have been properly fit tested and maintained. As noted above, NIOSH-certified respirators are marked with the manufacturer's name, the part number, the protection provided by the filter, and "NIOSH."

Employees who will be exposed to respiratory hazards other than airborne infectious agents (e.g., gases) should consult the *NIOSH Respirator Selection Logic* for more detailed guidance on appropriate respiratory protection at http://www.cdc.gov/niosh/docs/2005-100/default.html.

Replacing Disposable Respirators

Once worn in the presence of an infectious patient, the respirator should be considered potentially contaminated with infectious material, and touching the outside of the device should be avoided. Upon leaving the patient's room, the disposable respirator should be removed and discarded, followed by proper hand hygiene.

If a sufficient supply of respirators is not available during a pandemic, healthcare facilities may consider reuse as long as the device has not been obviously soiled or damaged (e.g., creased or torn), and it retains its ability to function properly. Data on reuse of respirators for infectious diseases are not available. Reuse may increase the potential for contamination; however, this risk must be balanced against the need to provide respiratory protection for healthcare workers.

Reuse of a disposable respirator should be limited to a single wearer (i.e., another wearer should not use the respirator). Consider labeling respirators with a user's name before use to prevent reuse by another individual.

If disposable respirators need to be reused by an individual user after caring for infectious patients, employers should implement a procedure for safe reuse to prevent contamination through contact with infectious materials on the outside of the respirator.

One way to address contamination of the respirator's exterior surface is to consider wearing a faceshield that does not interfere with the fit or seal over the respirator. Wearers should remove the barrier upon leaving the patient's room and perform hand hygiene. Face shields should be cleaned and disinfected. After removing the respirator, either hang it in a designated area or place it in a bag. Store the respirator in a manner that prevents its physical and functional integrity from being compromised.

In addition, use care when placing a used respirator on the face to ensure proper fit for respiratory protection and to avoid unnecessary contact with infectious material that may be present on the outside of the mask. Perform hand hygiene after replacing the respirator on the face.

Exhalation Valves

Some filtering facepiece (and all elastomeric) respirators come equipped with an exhalation valve, which can reduce the physiologic burden on the user by reducing the resistance during exhalation. An exhalation valve may also increase the user's comfort by reducing excessive dampness and warmth in the mask from exhaled breath. The valve opens to release exhaled breath and closes during inhalation so that inhaled air comes through the filter. Healthcare workers may wear respirators with exhalation valves unless the patient has a medical condition (such as an open wound) for which a healthcare worker would normally wear a surgical mask to protect the patient. Similarly, respirators with exhalation valves should not be placed on a patient to contain droplets and prevent spread of infectious particles; surgical masks can be used for this purpose.

Powered Air-Purifying Respirators

Powered air-purifying respirators use HEPA filters, which are as efficient as P100 filters and will protect against airborne infectious agents. Powered air-purifying respirators provide a higher level of protection than disposable respirators. Healthcare facilities have used higher levels of respiratory protection, including powered air-purifying respirators, for persons present during aerosol-generating medical procedures, such as bronchoscopy, on patients with infectious pulmonary diseases. When powered air-purifying respirators are used, their reusable elements should be cleaned and disinfected after use and the filters replaced in accordance with the manufacturer's recommendations. All used filters should be considered potentially contaminated with infectious material and must be safely discarded. Powered air-purifying respirators may also increase the comfort for some users by reducing the physiologic burden associated with negative pressure respirators and providing a constant flow of air on the face. In addition, there is no need for fit testing of loose-fitting hood or helmet models.

Special Considerations for Pandemic Preparedness

If employers prepare appropriately, respiratory protection against pandemic influenza will be more effective. Establishment of a comprehensive respiratory protection program with all of the elements specified in OSHA's Respiratory Protection standard (29 CFR 1910.134) is needed to achieve the highest levels of protection. (See the section OSHA Standards of Special Importance on page 50 and Appendix C-1 of this document) Acquiring adequate supplies of appropriate respirators, ensuring that they fit key personnel, conducting appropriate training, and performing other aspects of respiratory protection can be accomplished in advance of a pandemic influenza outbreak. These measures should be repeated annually, prior to a pandemic being declared, to assure continued preparedness.

If this is done, and the virus has an element of airborne transmission, the likelihood that employees will be effectively protected will be increased.

- Protection against pandemic influenza requires a comprehensive approach that includes both hygienic practices (e.g., handwashing and cough etiquette) and respiratory protection.
- Surgical masks are not considered adequate respiratory protection for airborne transmission of pandemic influenza. However, FDA-cleared surgical masks are fluid resistant and may be used for barrier protection against splashes and large droplets.
- Respiratory protection requires the use of a NIOSH-certified respirator and implementation of a comprehensive respiratory protection program that considers the following:
  - Use NIOSH-certified respirators that are N95 or higher. When both fluid protection (e.g., blood splashes) and respiratory protection are needed, use a "surgical N95" respirator that has been certified by NIOSH and cleared by the FDA.
  - Consider elastomeric respirators for essential employees who may have to decontaminate and reuse respirators in the event that there is a shortage of disposable respirators.
  - Consider powered air-purifying respirators for essential employees who may have to decontaminate and reuse respirators, wear respirators for prolonged periods of time, be exposed to high-risk procedures (e.g., bronchoscopy), or work in high-risk environments. Loose-fitting hooded powered air-purifying respirators have the additional advantage of not requiring fit testing.
- Employers, especially those whose employees are likely to be highly exposed to the flu virus (e.g., healthcare workers), should develop and implement a plan, train employees, and purchase/stockpile respiratory protection in advance for use during a pandemic since there will likely be shortages of necessary equipment during a real pandemic.

For more information regarding the use of respirators and surgical masks during a pandemic see, *Interim Guidance on Planning for the Use of Surgical Masks and Respirators in Health Care Settings during an Influenza Pandemic* at http://www.pandemicflu.gov/plan/healthcare/maskguidancehc.html.

PPE for Aerosol-Generating Procedures

During procedures that may generate increased small-particle aerosols of respiratory secretions, healthcare personnel should wear gloves, gowns, face/eye protection, and N95 respirators, surgical N95 respirators or other appropriate particulate respirators. Respirators must be used within the context of a respiratory protection program that includes a written program, fit testing, medical clearance, and training (see the section OSHA Standards of Special Importance and Appendix C-1 for more information). Consider the use of an airborne isolation room when conducting aerosol-generating procedures, whenever possible.[4]

Examples of procedures that generate aerosols include:[6]

- Endotracheal intubation
- Aerosolized or nebulized medication administration
- Diagnostic sputum induction
- Bronchoscopy
- Airway suctioning
- Positive pressure ventilation via face mask (e.g., BiPAP and CPAP)
- High-frequency oscillatory ventilation

Additional procedures that may result in aerosolization of respiratory secretions are listed in the World Health Organization (WHO) document, *Avian Influenza, including Influenza A (H5N1), in Humans: WHO Interim Infection Control Guideline for Health Care Facilities* Annex 4 at http://www.who.int/csr/disease/avian_influenza/guidelines/infectioncontrol1/en/.

Order for Putting on and Removing PPE

Based on the risk assessment, several items of PPE may be needed by healthcare workers when entering the room of a patient infected with known or suspected pandemic influenza.

When PPE is necessary for the specific situation, HHS/CDC recommends that personal protective equipment be put on in the following order:[38]

- Gown
- Respirator (or mask, when appropriate)
- Face shield or goggles
- Gloves

Upon leaving the room, HHS/CDC recommends that PPE be removed in a way to avoid self-contamination, as follows:[38]

- Gloves
- Faceshield or goggles

- Gown
- Respirator or mask

Remember to always use hand hygiene after removing PPE. A printable poster on the sequences for putting on and taking off PPE, which can be used for employee training and can be posted outside respiratory isolation rooms, is available at http://www.cdc.gov/ncidod/sars/ic.htm.

Work Practices

Hand Hygiene
To reduce the risk of becoming infected with influenza, healthcare workers working with influenza patients should follow rigorous hand hygiene measures. The HHS/CDC *Guideline for Hand Hygiene in Healthcare Settings* provides the recommendations for hand hygiene and the scientific support for the recommendations at http://www.cdc.gov/handhygiene.

Basic hand hygiene recommendations that help protect healthcare workers working with influenza patients are:[3, 4]

- Healthcare facilities should ensure that sinks with warm and cold running water, plain or antimicrobial soap, disposable paper towels, and alcohol-based hand disinfectants are readily accessible in areas where patient care is provided.
- When hands are visibly dirty or contaminated with respiratory secretions, wash hands with soap (either non-antimicrobial or antimicrobial) and water.
- When washing hands with soap and water, wet hands first with water, apply the amount of product recommended by the manufacturer to hands, and rub hands together vigorously for at least 15 seconds, covering all surfaces of the hands and fingers. Rinse hands with water and dry thoroughly with a disposable towel. Use a disposable towel to turn off the faucet.
- If hands are not visibly soiled, use an alcohol-based hand rub for routinely decontaminating hands in all clinical situations including contact, whether gloved or ungloved, with an influenza patient.
- When decontaminating hands with an alcohol-based hand rub, apply product to the palm of one hand and rub hands together, covering all surfaces of hands and fingers, until hands are dry. Follow the manufacturer's recommendations regarding the amount of product to use.
- Always use hand hygiene after removing gloves and other PPE.
- Healthcare facility leaders should make adherence to hand hygiene an institutional priority.

Other Hygienic Measures
Healthcare workers working with pandemic influenza patients should also take care to:[4]

- Avoid touching their eyes, nose, or mouth with contaminated hands (gloved or ungloved) to avoid self-inoculation with the pandemic influenza virus.
- Avoid contaminating environmental surfaces that are not directly related to patient care such as light switches and doorknobs.

Facility Hygiene—Practices and Polices
When handling supplies and equipment contaminated with blood and other potentially infectious materials, employees must comply with OSHA's Bloodborne Pathogens standard.

Dishes and Eating Utensils
Standard precautions are recommended for handling dishes and eating utensils used by a patient with known or suspected pandemic influenza.[4]

- Healthcare workers, including housekeeping staff, should wear gloves when handling pandemic influenza patients' trays, dishes, and utensils.
- The healthcare facility should wash reusable dishes and utensils in a dishwasher at the recommended water temperature.
- If disposable dishes and utensils are used, these may be discarded with other general waste.

For information regarding recommended water temperatures, consult the *Guidelines for Environmental Infection Control in Health-Care Facilities* at http://www.cdc.gov/ncidod/dhqp/gl_environinfection.html.

Linens and Laundry
The following precautions are recommended for handling linens and laundry that might be contaminated with respiratory secretions from patients with pandemic influenza:[4]

- Healthcare workers should place soiled linen directly into a laundry bag in the patient's room. The linen should be contained in a manner that prevents the bag from opening during transport and while in the soiled linen holding area.

- Healthcare workers should wear gloves and gowns when directly handling soiled linen and laundry (e.g., bedding, towels, and personal clothing), as per standard precautions. There should be no shaking or handling of soiled linen and laundry in a manner that might create an opportunity for disease transmission or contamination of the environment.
- Healthcare workers should wear gloves when transporting bagged linen and laundry.
- Healthcare workers should perform hand hygiene after removing gloves that have been in contact with soiled linen and laundry.
- The healthcare facility should ensure that linens and laundry are washed and dried in accordance with infection control standards and procedures.

For additional information, see the section Laundry and Bedding, in *Guidelines for Environmental Control in Health-Care Facilities* at http://www.cdc.gov/ncidod/dhqp/gl_environinfection.html.

Patient Care Equipment

To protect healthcare workers, standard practices for handling and reprocessing used patient care equipment, including medical devices, should be followed.[4]

- Healthcare workers should wear gloves when handling and transporting used patient care equipment.
- Healthcare workers should wipe heavily soiled equipment with a U.S. Environmental Protection Agency (EPA)-approved hospital disinfectant before removing it from the patient's room and follow current recommendations for cleaning and disinfection or sterilization of reusable patient care equipment.
- Healthcare workers should wipe external surfaces of portable equipment (e.g., for performing x-rays and other procedures) in the patient's room with an EPA-approved hospital disinfectant upon removal from the patient's room.

For additional information, see the section Environmental Services, in *Guidelines for Environmental Control in Health-Care Facilities* at http://www.cdc.gov/ncidod/dhqp/gl_environinfection.html.

Environmental Cleaning and Disinfection

Healthcare workers should use precautions when cleaning the rooms of pandemic influenza patients or of influenza patients who have been discharged or transferred.[4]

Cleaning and Disinfection of Patient-Occupied Rooms

- Wear gloves in accordance with facility policies for environmental cleaning.[4]
- Wear a surgical mask in accordance with droplet precautions.[4] Use a respirator when airborne precautions are warranted by the circumstances.
- Gowns are usually not necessary for routine cleaning of an influenza patient's room.[4] However, a gown must be worn when cleaning a patient's room if soiling of the employee's clothes or uniform with blood or other potentially infectious materials may occur.
- Wear face and eye protection if cleaning within 3 feet of a coughing patient.
- Keep areas within 3 feet of the patient free of unnecessary supplies and equipment to facilitate daily cleaning.[4]
- Use any EPA-registered hospital detergent-disinfectant.[4]
- Give special attention to frequently touched surfaces (e.g., bedrails, bedside and over-bed tables, TV controls, call buttons, telephones, lavatory surfaces including safety/pull-up bars, doorknobs, commodes, and ventilator surfaces) in addition to floors and other horizontal surfaces.[4]

Cleaning and Disinfection after Patient Discharge or Transfer [4]

- Follow standard facility procedures for post-discharge cleaning of an isolation room.
- Clean and disinfect all surfaces that were in contact with the patient or might have become contaminated during patient care.

Disposal of Solid Waste [4]

Standard precautions are recommended by HHS for disposal of solid waste (medical and non-medical) that might be contaminated with a pandemic influenza virus.

- Contain and dispose of contaminated medical waste in accordance with facility procedures and/or local or state regulations for handling and disposal of medical waste, including used needles and other sharps, and non-medical waste.
- Discard used patient care supplies that are not likely to be contaminated (e.g., paper wrappers) as routine waste.
- Healthcare workers should wear disposable gloves when handling waste and should practice hand hygiene after removal of gloves.

Laboratory Practices

Follow standard facility and laboratory practices for the collection, handling, and processing of laboratory specimens.[4] Follow airborne precautions when engaging in aerosol-generating procedures for specimen collection, such as diagnostic sputum induction.

References

[1] HHS. Centers for Disease Control and Prevention, Atlanta, Georgia. Garner JS, Hospital Infection Control Practices Advisory Committee. Guideline for isolation precautions in hospitals. Infect Control Hosp Epidemiol 1996; 17:53-80.

[2] Garner JS, Guideline for isolation precautions in hospitals. Part I. Evolution of isolation practices, Hospital Infection Control Practices Advisory Committee. Am J Infect Control 1996; 24:24-52.

[3] HHS. Centers for Disease Control and Prevention (CDC) Guideline for Hand Hygiene in Health-Care Settings. MMWR. October 25, 2002/51 (RR16); 1-44.

[4] HHS. 2005. Pandemic Influenza Plan, Supplement 4. U.S. Department of Health and Human Services. Last accessed February 20, 2005: www.hhs.gov/pandemicflu/plan/sup4.html.

[5] CDC, Interim Recommendations for Infection Control in Healthcare Facilities Caring for Patients with Known or Suspected Avian Influenza, May 21, 2004, http://www.cdc.gov/flu/avian/professional/infect-control.htm.

[6] HHS. CDC, Public Health Guidance for Community-Level Preparedness and Response to Severe Acute Respiratory Syndrome (SARS) Version 2 Supplement I: Infection Control in Healthcare, Home, and Community Settings, III. Infection Control in Healthcare Facilities May 3, 2005 accessed 4/11/2006 at http://www.cdc.gov/ nci-dod/sars/guidance/I/healthcare.htm.

[7] HHS. Centers for Disease Control and Prevention (CDC) Guidelines for the Prevention of Health-Care-Associated Pneumonia. MMWR, March 26, 2004 / 53(RR-03);1-36.

[8] HHS. Interim Guidance on Planning for the Use of Surgical Masks and Respirators in Health Care Settings during an Influenza Pandemic. October 2006. Accessed 3/7/07 at www.pandemicflu.gov/plan/healthcare/maskguidancehc.html.

[9] Kellerman SE, Saiman L, San Gabriel P, Besser R, Jarvis WR. Observational study of the use of infection control interventions for Mycobacterium tuberculosis in pediatric facilities. Pediatr Infect Dis J. 2001 Jun;20(6):566-70.

[10] Ofner-Agostini, et al., Cluster of Cases of Severe Acute Respiratory Syndrome Among Toronto Healthcare Workers After Implementation of Infection Control Precautions: A Case Series Infect Control Hosp Epidemiol 2006; 27: 473-478.

[11] HHS. Public Health Service, Centers for Disease Control and Prevention, National Institute for Occupational Safety and Health, TB Respiratory Protection Program in Health Care Facilities Administrator's Guide, September 1999.

[12] Imai, et al., SARS risk perceptions in healthcare workers, Japan. Emerg Infect Disease 2005; 11: 404-410.

[13] Gershon RRM, et al. Compliance with universal precautions among health care workers at three regional hospitals. Am J Infect Control 1995;23:225-36.

[14] DeJoy DM, et al. The influence of employee, job/task, and organizational factors on adherence to universal precautions among nurses. Int J Ind Ergon 1995;16:43-55.

[15] DeJoy DM, et al. Behavioral-diagnostic analysis of compliance with universal precautions among nurses. J Occup Health Psychol 2000;5:127-41.

[16] Gershon RR, et al. Hospital safety climate and its relationship with safe work practices and workplace exposure incidents. Am J Infect Control 2000;28: 211-21.

[17] SARS Key Learnings from the Perspective of University Health Network, Notes for the Campbell Commission, Available at: http://www.uhn.ca/uhn/corporate/community/docs/campbell_presentation_100103.pdf.

[18] HHS. Pandemic Influenza Plan, Part 1, Strategic Plan, November 2005 Available at http://www.hhs.gov/pandemicflu/plan/part1.html.

[19] Loutfy, et al., Hospital Preparedness and SARS, Emerg Inf Dis, Vol. 10, No. 5, May 2004. p 771-776.

[20] Centers for Disease Control and Prevention, Instructions to Estimate the Potential Impact of the Next Influenza Pandemic Upon Locale Y, Available at http://www.cdc.gov/flu/pandemic/impactestimate.htm; accessed 6/19/06.

[21] National Strategy for Pandemic Influenza: Implementation Plan, November 2005, Available at http://www.whitehouse.gov/homeland/pandemic-influenza-implementation.html.

[22] AHA Hospital Statistics 2006 edition, Health Forum LLC.

[23] Mead K, Johnson D. An evaluation of portable high-efficiency particulate air filtration for expedient patient isolation in epidemic and emergency response. Ann Emerg Med 2004; 44: 635-645.

[24] Rosenbaum R, et al., Use of a portable forced air system to convert existing hospital space into a mass casualty isolation area. Ann Emerg Med 2004; 44: 628-634.

[25] Biosafety in Microbiological and Biomedical Laboratories (BMBL), 4th edition, May, 1999, http://bmbl.od.nih.gov/, accessed 6/23/06.

[26] HHS. Pandemic Influenza Plan Supplement 2 Laboratory Diagnostics. Available at http://www.hhs.gov/pandemicflu/plan/sup2.html.

[27] State Public Health Laboratories Emergency Contact List November 2005. Available at http://www.asm.org/ASM/files/LeftMarginHeaderList/DOWNLOADFILENAME/000000000527/LabState Contacts.pdf.

[28] World Health Organization. Avian Influenza, including Influenza A (H5N1), in Humans: WHO Interim Infection Control Guideline for Health Care Facilities. Revised April 24, 2006. Accessed on August 23, 2006 at http://www.who.int/csr/disease/avian_influenza/guidelines/infectioncontrol1/en/.

[29] CDC. Public Health Guidance for Community Level Preparedness and Response to Severe Acute Respiratory Syndrome (SARS) January 8, 2004, Supplement C: Preparedness and Response in Healthcare Facilities, pp. 1-34., Available at: http://www.cdc.gov/NCIDOD/SARS/guidance/C/index.htm.

[30] SARS Commission Interim Report SARA and Public Health in Ontario, April 15, 2004, http://www.sarscommission.ca/report/Interim_Report.pdf.

[31] HHS. 2005. Pandemic Influenza Plan. Part II. Sup 7. November.

[32] HHS. 2005. Pandemic Influenza Plan, Appendix D. U.S. Department of Health and Human Services. Last accessed March 21, 2006: www.hhs.gov/pandemicflu/plan/appendixd.html.

[33] Centers for Disease Control and Prevention (CDC). Interventions to increase influenza vaccination of healthcare workers—California and Minnesota. MMWR Morb Mortal Wkly Rep. 4;54(8):196-9, Mar 2005. www.cdc.gov/mmwr/preview/mmwrhtml/mm5408a2.htm.

[34] HHS. 2005. Pandemic Influenza Plan. Part II. Sup 6. November.

[35] Varia, M, et al. Investigation of a nosocomial outbreak of severe acute respiratory syndrome (SARS) in Toronto, Canada. CMAJ 2003; 169(4):285-292.

[36] Chen CC, Willeke K. Aerosol penetration through surgical masks. Am J Infect Control 1992; 20(4):177-184.

[37] Derrick JL, Gomersall CD. Protecting healthcare staff from severe acute respiratory syndrome: filtration capacity of multiple surgical masks. J Hosp Infect 2005; 59(4):365-368.

[38] HHS. CDC Poster: Sequence for Donning and Removing Personal Protective Equipment (PPE) (May 7, 2004) accessed 4/11/2006 at http://www.cdc.gov/ncidod/sars/ic.htm.

Pandemic Influenza Preparedness

An influenza pandemic is projected to have a worldwide impact on morbidity and mortality, thus requiring a sustained, large-scale response that has the potential to quickly overwhelm hospitals and the healthcare system regionally and nationally. Because an influenza pandemic may quickly overwhelm the healthcare community (hospitals, outpatient clinics, the pre-hospital environment, nursing homes, assisted living centers, and private home healthcare) planning should address: (1) internal continuation of care and (2) coordination of services with local, state, and federal healthcare agencies. Healthcare resources are not easily shared or redistributed; a pandemic will magnify and strain resources on a much larger scale. Collaboration with state and federal partners is vital to ensure that healthcare facilities have assistance with consumables, medication, and vaccines during the pandemic.[1,2,3]

This section addresses pandemic planning issues affecting healthcare personnel, the most valuable resource in a pandemic crisis.[1,2,3] It is beyond the scope of this document to give specific details on resource management for individual healthcare settings. Instead, comprehensive planning for these issues, such as surge capacity, facility space management, and consumable and durable equipment utilization should be developed in coordination with local, state, and federal agencies. There are several checklists, toolkits, and guidelines that will assist healthcare providers and service organizations in planning for a pandemic outbreak available at http://www.pandemicflu.gov/plan/healthcare/index.html. For additional influenza pandemic planning resources, see the Appendix section of this document.

Healthcare Facility Responsibilities During Pandemic Alert Periods

In the event of a pandemic, HHS/CDC will coordinate support and intelligence with U.S. public health departments regarding the pandemic situation in the U.S. and in foreign countries. The Homeland Security Council (HSC) National Strategy for Pandemic Influenza Implementation Plan has identified stages for federal government actions during a pandemic. The stages are based on spread of the virus in other countries and in the United States. These stages can be incorporated into healthcare pandemic planning to identify triggers for implementation of different aspects of the facility plan. Below is a broad outline of pandemic planning for healthcare facilities based on stages of the Homeland Security Council National Strategy for Pandemic Influenza Implementation Plan and the HHS *Pandemic Influenza Plan* recommendations.[14]

Healthcare Facility Responsibilities Before a Pandemic (HSC Stages 0, 1)

- Develop planning and decision making strategies for responding to pandemic influenza.
  - Define roles for disaster response, including responsibility for coordination of a pandemic plan. For example, identify the individuals within your organization who will be responsible for coordinating communications, integrating public health recommendations, establishing security, and developing a written plan.
  - Note that individual circumstances may affect specific facilities (e.g., rural vs. urban medical facilities, hospital vs. pre-hospital and general practices vs. specialized medical facilities).
- Understand how to access state and federal information and supplies, and to ensure communication with local, state, and federal health and security agencies. Identify supply chain issues and develop alternatives as needed (e.g., overseas sources).
- Develop written plans that address disease surveillance, isolation and quarantine practices, hospital capacity criteria, hospital communication, staff education and training, triage, clinical evaluation and diagnosis, security, facility access, facility infrastructure (e.g., isolation rooms), occupational health for employees, use and administration of vaccines and antiviral drugs, facility surge capacity (e.g., durable and consumable supplies), supply chains (purchase, distribution and transportation of supplies), access to critical inventory supplies, and mortuary issues (e.g., storage capacity). This is not a comprehensive list. Planning should be tailored to the specific facility and community.
- Work with local, state and national emergency planning committees to integrate with community, state and national pandemic plans and training.
- Participate in pandemic influenza response exercises and drills on local and, if possible, state and federal levels. Incorporate lessons learned into the pandemic disaster response plans.

Healthcare Facility Responsibilities During the Pandemic (HSC Stages 2 – 5)

If there are confirmed human outbreaks overseas (Stages 2 – 3):

- Heighten institutional surveillance of patients and facility/clinic staff for influenza-like illness.
- Prepare to activate institutional pandemic influenza plans, as necessary.
- Establish communications with local, state, and federal agencies regarding surveillance issues and recommendations.

If pandemic influenza begins in or enters the United States (Stages 4 – 5):[4]

- Activate institutional pandemic influenza plans to protect staff and patients.
- Heighten institutional surveillance of patients and facility/clinic staff for influenza-like illness.
- Implement surge capacity plans to sustain healthcare delivery.
- Identify and isolate potential pandemic influenza patients.
- Implement infection control practices to prevent influenza transmission and monitor staff and patients for nosocomial transmission.
- Ensure rapid and frequent communication within healthcare facilities and between healthcare facilities, state health departments, and the federal government.
- Ensure that there is a process for reporting influenza cases and fatalities.

Healthcare Facility Recovery and Preparation for Subsequent Pandemic Waves (HSC Stage 6)

- Continue institutional surveillance of patients and facility/clinic staff for influenza-like illness.
- Return to normal facility operations as soon as possible.
- Review pandemic influenza plan based on experience during the first pandemic wave. Incorporate lessons learned into preparation for subsequent pandemic waves.
- Identify and anticipate resource and supply chain issues.
- Continue to emphasize communication within healthcare facilities and between healthcare facilities, state health departments, and the federal government to identify subsequent pandemic waves.

Incorporating Pandemic Plans into Disaster Plans

Hospitals already address emergency management plans as part of the Joint Commission on Accreditation of Healthcare Organizations (JCAHO) standards. Standards EC.4.10 and EC4.20 address emergency management and require hospitals to conduct a hazard vulnerability analysis as a first step in disaster planning. A hazard vulnerability analysis allows hospitals to assess the type, probability, impact, and severity of specific hazards and disasters. This information allows hospitals to anticipate the effects of these events and facilitates customized planning and resource stockpiling. Specific information on conducting a hazard vulnerability analysis can be obtained though the Joint Commission Resources, an affiliate of JCAHO.[5, 6]

In 2003, the National Hospital Ambulatory Medical Care Survey reported that about 97 percent of surveyed hospitals had plans for responding to natural disasters and 85 percent had plans to respond to bioterrorism events. Although 75.9 percent reported cooperative planning with other facilities, only 46.1 percent had written Memoranda of Understanding regarding acceptance of patients during a disaster. The survey revealed that hospitals drilled for natural disasters more than for terrorism events and drilled even less for severe epidemics.[7] Despite recommendations and requirements for disaster planning, some institutions may be unprepared for a pandemic event. To address this concern, healthcare institutions should consider incorporating pandemic influenza planning into disaster planning by developing an algorithm that would group biologic agents with similar characteristics (i.e., smallpox, plague, influenza, severe acute respiratory syndrome (SARS)).[3] Plans should address some key differences in biological disaster plans and influenza pandemic plans.

Pandemic Planning for Support of Healthcare Worker Staff

Although a pandemic will be a nationwide event, it will be experienced on a local level. An important difference between pandemic planning and mass casualty planning is the understanding that during an influenza pandemic, hospital staff will be a limited resource, without an opportunity for replenishment from other communities. Plans must address protection of this vital and critical resource. Planning assumptions in the *National Strategy for Pandemic Influenza Implementation Plan* include a 30 percent attack rate in the U.S. population, 50

Influenza Pandemic Planning Issues

- Healthcare facilities may have more warning time and response time for pandemic influenza, especially if the initial outbreak develops in another country. Mass casualty and weapons of mass destruction events are typically a surprise.
- Influenza pandemic is not a contained or local event. Since it is widespread, less federal, state and local support is available at the individual facility level.
- Unlike a mass casualty or weapons of mass destruction event, emphasis on cohorting practices, isolation practices, and sterilization procedures is more important for pandemic infection control than decontamination.
- An influenza pandemic is a sustained crisis. Expect the response to have a longer duration (12 to 24 months).
- Unlike an isolated mass casualty scenario, a pandemic may come and go in waves, each of which can last for six to eight weeks.
- Prevention options (vaccine) and treatment options (medications) are fewer and more uncertain for pandemic influenza. A vaccine will likely not be available early in the pandemic. Antiviral medication is in short supply, is highly susceptible to resistance, and may not be effective.
- Due to the uncertainty of the nature of pandemic, pandemic plans must be flexible with integrated processes for reviewing current recommendations and updating the plan accordingly.

percent of those ill will seek medical attention, and an absenteeism rate of up to 40 percent. For information regarding planning assumptions, see http://www.pandemicflu.gov/plan/pandplan.html. These assumptions could also be adapted for local pandemic planning purposes to address hospital staffing shortages and surge requirements.[1]

Define Essential Staff and Hospital Services

Defining essential staff and services is typically one of the first and most vital steps in pandemic planning. During a pandemic, non-pandemic hospital services such as trauma care, obstetrics, cardiac care, and psychiatry will still need to be provided or a referral service made available. Hospitals need to identify crucial administrative staff, food services staff, housekeeping, security, and facilities staff. Once these essential personnel and positions are identified, consider implementing cross-training to ensure that these processes will continue. Also, identify and develop methods and policies in compliance with federal, state and local requirements for keeping nonessential staff out of the facility such as through reassignment, administrative leave or furlough policies. However, even if an individual's position is considered nonessential, these personnel may be cross-trained and utilized as a contingency workforce.[3, 4, 8, 9, 10]

Physicians and nurses with crucial knowledge of infectious disease, pulmonary medicine and critical care medicine will need to be identified. Nurses are currently an understaffed profession; in a pandemic situation, this shortage will be even more pronounced. Consider how to maximize nursing care by estimating the number of staff needed to care for a single patient or multiple patients, and then plan how to meet those needs when there is an increase in patients or a decrease in staff. Medical and nursing students may be a potential resource to meet staffing shortages and to extend care. The HHS *Pandemic Influenza Plan* advises that patients' family members could be used in an ancillary healthcare capacity. Identify other critical care personnel such as respiratory therapists, pharmacists, laboratory employees, blood bank and morgue staff. To prepare for staffing shortages, consider cross-training staff for essential areas such as the emergency department or intensive care units.[4, 8, 9, 10]

Essential Personnel and Processes

- Designate a multidisciplinary planning committee responsible for pandemic preparedness and response.
- Empower managers and planners with the authority and resources to formulate policies, implement training and enforce work practices to protect employees and patients.
- Identify essential facility staffing and functions.
- Recognize deficiencies such as potential staffing shortages, lack of written guidelines and develop targets for improvement.
- Prepare contingency plans to address critical services.
- Cross-train individuals for leadership roles and to identify a contingency workforce.

Human Resources

Hospital staff and healthcare workers will be a limited resource during a pandemic influenza outbreak due to illness and/or absenteeism. There will be a need for people with healthcare training, of any level, to meet the increased demands on the local healthcare community. Begin working with other facilities and clinics to develop Memorandums of Understanding for staffing support. Work with these medical clinics to ensure that healthcare workers in the community are aware of institution planning, protocols and training. Provide communication infrastructure to ensure that practitioners in the community have the resources to integrate with larger facilities.[1, 4, 8]

Healthcare employers should be prepared to support existing employees and to accommodate an influx of new providers, both volunteers and recruited individuals. Healthcare facilities should work with JCAHO and state medical boards to ensure an expedited but legal credentialing process. A potential resource for personnel augmentation is state Emergency Systems for Advance Registration of Health Professions Volunteers (ESAR-VHP). These state systems are being developed in partnership with HHS to register, classify and verify credentials of potential health professional volunteers in each state (http://www.hrsa.gov/esarvhp/) Local Medical Reserve Corps units may also be sources of volunteer health professional personnel in the immediate vicinity of a facility (http://www.medicalreservecorps.gov/HomePage).[1, 4]

Pandemic influenza planners should also address workers' compensation issues in advance, including workplace injuries and illness to volunteers and new recruits working in response to a pandemic. Experience during the SARS outbreak showed that wages and salary issues may also arise as healthcare workers are requested to work with infectious cases.[8, 9] Workplace issues arising in the context of a pandemic (e.g., reassignment, payment of wages or salaries, voluntary or involuntary sick leave, delegation of work duties) should be resolved in compliance with federal, state, and local laws, including equal employment opportunity laws.

Human resources should be involved in planning for other employee support concerns such as the possible need for housing, meals, places to rest, and child care services. Prepare and plan how the healthcare facility will provide these services in planning stages so that during a crisis, employees will already have this information.[11]

> ### Human Resources
> - Identify community volunteer and available medical support professionals.
> - Develop processes for training, credentialing, and communicating with community professionals.
> - Plan for health and compensation concerns of healthcare workers.

Information Technology

During a pandemic situation, communication capabilities to provide risk communications internal and external to facilities are essential. Adequate communication infrastructure (computers, Internet, and radios) will ensure that providers, patients and community resources can exchange accurate, timely information about the situation. Equipment should be tested to ensure compatibility with emergency services, law enforcement, security and public health. Inability to communicate effectively because of technology incompatibility could result in further strain on the healthcare system and healthcare workers.[12, 13, 14]

It is anticipated that during an influenza pandemic the members of the healthcare community will increase their reliance on information technologies. Quarantine requirements during the SARS outbreak made it difficult for hospital staff to receive current information about the outbreak situation, particularly changing treatment strategies, and recommendations for personal protective measures. The cancellation of medical rounds and business meetings further exacerbated the lack of personal communications. E-mail, telephone conferences, and Internet access enabled healthcare providers to access treatment specialists external to the facility, and obtain the information required to maintain the most current standards of care from public health experts. Once these processes were in place, healthcare providers were able to address effective patient treatment and personal protective measures. Pandemic planning should address the anticipated increased reliance on information technologies and ensure that the communication infrastructure enables healthcare workers to access the most current recommendations.[4, 8, 9, 10, 12, 13, 14, 15]

Public Health Communications

Healthcare facilities need to develop strong risk communications resources as part of pandemic planning for both the community that they serve and their employees. Risk communications should be available in formats accessible to individuals with disabilities and/or limited English proficiency, and should also target the educational level of the intended audience.

Communication with the community, including public relations and risk communications, will be required to ensure that the general public is educated in self-care techniques, social distancing and access to the appropriate level of care.[15] Healthcare facilities and outpatient clinics should consider telephone hotlines and websites to provide health advice to the public. Hotlines and websites can educate the public in self-care or direct ill individuals to the appropriate level of care and decrease the burden on healthcare facilities. Healthcare facilities and clinics can also institute follow-up phone or e-mail communication to ensure that discharged or home-care patients are adequately managed.[1, 4, 15]

HHS has developed resources for avian influenza and pandemic influenza communications using the communication science-based message mapping development process. "Message maps" are risk communications tools used to help organize complex information and make it easier to express current knowledge. The development process distills information into easily understood messages written at a sixth grade reading level. These pandemic influenza and avian influenza message maps may be copied and redistributed on paper or electronically (http://www.pandemicflu.gov/rcommunication/pre_event_maps.pdf).

During a pandemic there will be rumors and misinformation that can impact healthcare staff and the community. Fraudulent information about counterfeit vaccines and antiviral medications may be circulated via multiple communication sources.[1, 16] Malicious misinformation may also be launched against local, state and federal agencies.[16] Without a reliable means to communicate accurate information, misinformation may adversely impact healthcare facilities and the public health infrastructure.

For additional information regarding public health communications see:

- Department of Health and Human Services *Pandemic Influenza Plan, Supplement 10*, available at http://www.hhs.gov/pandemicflu/plan/sup10.html#I.
- Pandemicflu.gov "Risk Communication" website, available at http://www.pandemicflu.gov/news/rcommunication.html.

Information Technology and Public Health Communications

- Develop information technology and communication infrastructure.
- Provide effective risk communication to staff and community.
- Consider implementing hotlines/websites to communicate with the public and employees.
- Identify misinformation and counter with timely, accurate information.
- Make communications available in formats accessible to individuals with disabilities and/or limited English proficiency, and also target the educational level of the intended audience.

Surveillance and Protocols

Surveillance is a cornerstone of disaster preparedness. Healthcare facilities and outpatient clinics both need to address and implement the capacity to identify and track influenza-like illness. This capability includes identifying appropriate laboratory capacity, the ability to conduct epidemiology on influenza-like illness and to report collected data to the appropriate state and federal agencies. Once a surveillance program is established, healthcare facilities will be able to identify the onset of a severe influenza season, identify biologic weapons (anthrax, plague, etc.) and monitor for pandemic influenza and/or other emerging respiratory infections (i.e., SARS, Hantavirus pulmonary syndrome). Healthcare facilities should conduct internal surveillance to monitor for nosocomial transmission of influenza to staff and other patients. Internal surveillance for nosocomial transmission could be used to identify inadequate infection control practices/procedures.[1, 12, 17, 18, 19]

Effective disease surveillance depends on cooperation with local, state, and federal health agencies to ensure that healthcare facilities have access to influenza diagnostic criteria, confirmatory laboratory tests, and an understanding of the reporting process in the event of an influenza pandemic. Health departments in all fifty states and Chicago, New York City and Washington, D.C. have dedicated influenza surveillance coordinators who promote year-round influenza surveillance. These are important resources for both hospitals and clinics. In the outpatient setting, the Sentinel Provider

Network (SPN) is a network of healthcare providers who report the number of weekly influenza-like illness visits and submit samples for testing. State public health departments can assist outpatient providers who wish to participate in the surveillance program. Healthcare facilities can participate in the Emerging Infections Program (EIP) and New Vaccine Surveillance Network (NVSN). Like the SPN, the EIP and NVSN are administered through state health departments and coordinated with federal agencies such as HHS/CDC. Information about participation in these surveillance activities is coordinated through state health departments.[1, 17] Healthcare organizations, hospitals and outpatient clinics at least should develop a process to monitor the following federal and global sources to obtain the latest information on seasonal influenza, avian influenza, pandemic influenza, and other novel respiratory illnesses:

- Department of Health and Human Services http://www.pandemicflu.gov/outbreaks/#ussurv.
- Centers for Disease Control and Prevention http://www.cdc.gov/flu/weekly/fluactivity.htm.
- World Health Organization http://www.who.int/csr/disease/influenza/influenzanetwork/en/index.html.

Another important aspect of pandemic planning is establishment of protocols for patient screening, treatment, and flow. Patients with influenza-like symptoms should be identified as quickly as possible. Planning should include contingencies to isolate patients with influenza-like illness from other patients and staff. Criteria should be developed for triage, admission, care, and discharge of patients. Additional protocols should be developed to address points of entry into a facility, screening of healthcare workers, pharmacy access, emergency medical services transport priority, altered standards of care, and procedures for handling the deceased. During the SARS epidemic, triage criteria and changing protocols were a source of confusion and stress for healthcare workers. Staff that are trained and comfortable with triage, admission, treatment and discharge criteria, experience reduced stress and provide quality patient care during a crisis.[4, 8, 11, 20]

Facilities should also develop visitor screening and access policies for a pandemic. If these policies are not developed in advance, visitor access becomes a security issue and a source of stress for staff, patients, and families. Visitor policies should address access to ill family members, particularly pediatric patients, and policies for visitation of deceased patients.[21] Visitation policies will be easi-

er for the public to accept if the justification and rationale are explained before a crisis.[4, 21]

Surveillance and Protocols

- Develop surveillance capabilities for influenza-like illness.
- Ensure infrastructure for reporting influenza cases to state and federal agencies.
- Develop protocols for transport, triage, admission, treatment, discharge and other patient services.
- Develop visitation policies for ill and deceased patients.

Psychological Support

Psychological and behavioral health support for hospital staff is a recommended part of pandemic planning.[11, 20, 22, 23, 24] Personnel will be exposed to public education and outreach with the potential for conflicting messages, public health surveillance efforts, and community containment strategies in addition to work-related efforts involving mass prophylaxis strategies, ethical dilemmas due to shortages of critical supplies and surges in demand for healthcare service, and possible work-related stigma or maladaptive responses of coworkers due to changes in work practices or loads. Pandemic planning should address numerous areas of potential distress, health risk behaviors, and psychiatric disease amongst healthcare system personnel.

The importance of psychological support for healthcare staff was illustrated during the SARS outbreak in Canada. During the initial outbreak in Toronto, there was a high perception of risk due to lack of information about infection control, morbidity and mortality.[8, 13, 14, 20, 25] Healthcare workers, particularly those working directly with SARS patients, reported feeling afraid, helpless, angry, guilty, and frustrated. One of study of nurses who treated SARS patients in Taiwan demonstrated an 11 percent rate of traumatic stress reactions, including depression, anxiety, hostility, and somatization symptoms.[26] However, despite the risk, healthcare workers in Toronto and Asia continued to report to work.[8, 13, 20]

The psychological impact of SARS was not only felt among personnel directly involved in caring for SARS patients, but also among hospital employees who were restricted from work either because they were not in essential positions or quarantined due to exposure or illness. Supervisors and employees reported feeling isolated and ineffective, and expressed relief when reassigned to duties in the facility. Reintegrating employees back into work was also difficult. Employees reported feeling disorganized and disconnected and reported some resentment between employees who had been required to work and those who had been removed.[11, 20]

The impact of treating SARS cases was not isolated to the workplace. In order to protect their families, healthcare workers often isolated themselves at home. Healthcare workers and their families reported experiencing ostracism outside the workplace and stated that people in the community were afraid to associate with them and their families.[8, 11]

Healthcare facilities should plan and implement psychological resources for hospital staff during and after a pandemic. If there are adequate resources, facilities should consider extending services to employee family members.[11] The following resources provide detailed recommendations for incorporating psychological support for healthcare workers and their families into pandemic planning:

- Supplement 11 of the HHS *Pandemic Influenza Plan* at www.hhs.gov/pandemicflu/plan/sup11.htm/.
- Center for the Study of Traumatic Stress. Mental Health and Behavioral Guidelines for Response to Pandemic Influenza. http://www.usuhs.mil/psy/CSTSPandemicAvianInfluenza.pdf

---

Psychological Support

- Incorporate psychological support of healthcare workers into pandemic planning.
- Reinforce to healthcare workers their value and importance to the community.
- Consider extending resources to cover families of healthcare workers.
- Psychological resources should be offered to healthcare workers for an extended time period after the pandemic crises has resolved.

Occupational Health Services

Identifying and collaborating with institutional occupational health services is vital to effective pandemic influenza planning. Occupational health services can coordinate and participate in a variety of pandemic influenza preparedness and response activities.

Developing and Providing Employee Screening for Influenza-Like Illness

Occupational health services can monitor employee absentee rates in both the pre-pandemic planning stages and during a pandemic in order to gauge the impact and progression of the pandemic on the facility and the community. In the event of an influenza pandemic, all staff should be screened for illness before contact with patients or other healthcare workers. Planning should include processes to screen employees, track ill healthcare staff and reintegrate staff back into the workplace after recovery.[4, 9, 27]

A sample screening form is available from the WHO document Influenza A (H5N1): WHO Interim Infection Control Guidelines for Healthcare Facilities, Annex 10 at http://www.who.int/csr/disease/avian_influenza/guidelinestopics/en/index3.html. The form screens employees for signs and symptoms of infection over multiple days, providing a mechanism to ensure that exposed individuals are symptom-free before contact with patients and staff.

Developing and Providing Immunization and Treatment Strategies

Occupational health services should be prepared to work with state and federal agencies in order to facilitate pandemic influenza vaccination for employees and the public. Healthcare facilities and organizations need be aware of and coordinate with state pandemic planners to assure access to available vaccine.[1, 4] The pandemic vaccine may require multiple doses, so occupational health services should develop a system to identify and record vaccination status for pandemic vaccine recipients.

In addition to a pandemic influenza vaccine planning strategy, a current, aggressive vaccination program against seasonal influenza is integral to institutional preparedness. An effective seasonal influenza program can be adapted for a pandemic vaccination campaign.[4]

Antiviral medication may be a treatment option for ill healthcare staff. To maximize effectiveness, these medications should be given as soon as possible within 48 hours of the onset of symptoms. Screening for appropriate, early treatment of influenza cases among healthcare workers and essential staff could decrease the duration and severity of staffing illness and absence. Occupational health services should also be prepared to treat secondary bacterial infections in healthcare workers. Treatment and prophylaxis recommendations will be determined by HHS, but planning for employee screening and treatment should be implemented during the pandemic process.[4, 27]

Continuing Baseline Occupational Health Services

During an influenza pandemic, protection against existing occupational hazards (e.g., bloodborne pathogens and tuberculosis) will need to continue. Pandemic influenza planning should include a process to quickly integrate volunteers and recruited staff into healthcare facilities to ensure that healthcare workers are adequately protected. Despite the demands of a pandemic, infection control practices will still need to be maintained. Bloodborne pathogens exposure control plans, respiratory protection programs, and tuberculosis screening must be continued during an influenza pandemic. New staff and volunteers should be included in these programs to ensure facility and employee safety and health.

ensure that protocols and resources for just-in-time training are in place. If possible, identify pools of back-up staff or volunteer staff and began training these individuals in infection control practices and respiratory protection (including fit testing) to ensure smooth integration in the healthcare facility in the event of a pandemic.

It is important to remember that patient care providers are not the only personnel that need pandemic preparedness training. For example, food services, housekeeping, information technologists, facility managers and human resources are critical functions and may require pandemic-specific training (i.e., hygiene practices).[4, 9]

Healthcare facilities should also consider developing training for families of employees. Ensuring that families of healthcare workers are educated about hygiene and disease can protect healthcare systems and reduce employee absence.[11]

JCAHO requirements include training and drills as part of disaster planning. Drilling for a pandemic situation ensures that facilities are prepared for surge capacity, supply chains, communication infrastructure, and adequate occupational safety and health protocols. Disaster drills allow planners to identify hidden complications that may arise in the event of a pandemic.[5, 6]

Occupational Health Services

- Incorporate institutional occupational health services into pandemic preparedness.
- Develop surveillance, screening and treatment protocols.
- Coordinate with local, state and federal agencies for access and recommendations for administration of antiviral medications and pandemic influenza vaccination.
- Ensure that all employees and volunteers are safely integrated into the healthcare facility.

Training

- Advance training is essential for facility pandemic preparedness.
- Identify critical functions and identify individuals for training in these functions.
- Infection control and use of PPE are appropriate training topics in pandemic preparedness planning.
- Disaster drills are an optimal approach to testing pandemic preparedness.
- Training should be available in formats accessible to individuals with disabilities and/or limited English proficiency, and should also target the educational level of the intended audience.

Training

Training for a pandemic is essential to ensure continued effective operation of the facility. Cross-training and volunteer training for essential functions should be initiated early in pandemic preparedness planning. If advance training is not an option, then

Security

A pandemic crisis will intensify the need for facility security. Security will be an essential function and additional personnel may be needed during a pandemic.[1, 2, 4] A pandemic will require facilities to limit access and implement isolation measures to separate potential cases from staff, visitors, and other patients. In a pandemic, healthcare facility security may need to be ready to address crowd control and physical protection of the facility and hospital staff.[4]

Security staff will be interfacing with a scared and potentially dangerous public. Not only will security personnel be at risk for infection, but they may have to confront violent individuals demanding resources and healthcare. Training and providing personal protective equipment (PPE) is essential for these hospital personnel. Facilities should incorporate training and support for security personnel in the pandemic planning process.

Healthcare facilities should also work with local and federal law enforcement agencies to address facility security. Consider preparing security plans with local and state law enforcement. This will allow law enforcement agencies to develop procedures for entrance to and egress of from the facility, public access issues, and protection of critical supplies. Ensure that law enforcement understands facility structure and layout in advance of a crisis. Identify key individuals to liaison with law enforcement agencies and coordinate planning and communications (i.e., radios). Without adequate security and the cooperation of law enforcement agencies, healthcare facilities may not be able to function during a crisis.

Security

- Security will be an essential requirement during a pandemic.
- Train security personnel on specific roles and pandemic scenarios.
- Ensure that security personnel have adequate infection control resources.
- Integrate facility security with local and state law enforcement agencies to ensure adequate protection and support of the healthcare facility and employees.
- Inform and train employees about expected security measures during a pandemic.

Stockpiles of Essential Resources

An issue that all healthcare facilities must address as part of pandemic planning is stockpiling resources. Due to logistic and economic concerns, this element of disaster planning is often neglected. In 2004, the state of Kentucky conducted a survey of mass casualty planning in healthcare facilities.

Thirty-eight percent of respondents had emergency plans that addressed stockpiling antibiotics and supplies and only 25 percent of hospitals actually had a separate cache of antibiotics for staff in the event of a bioterrorist event.[28]

Influenza pandemic planning adds additional challenges for disaster stockpiling. An influenza pandemic will be sustained and widespread, and pharmaceutical interventions are currently in short supply or nonexistent. These factors limit the ability of facilities to stockpile pandemic resources. For this reason, healthcare facilities should ensure that pandemic plans address the ability to access local, state and federal stockpiles. Integration with these resources is vital to ensure distribution and rotation of essential supplies during a crisis.[1, 3, 4, 29]

HHS has recommended that healthcare facilities consider developing institutional stockpiles of resources to counter supply shortages and transportation issues that may impact the ability to access federal and state supplies.[4] JCAHO disaster guidance recommends that hospitals have a 48-to-72 hour stand-alone capability;[30] however, an influenza pandemic may surge through a community for 6 to 8 weeks. Consequently, stockpile planning will have to balance economic and logistical demands with the duration of pandemic waves and healthcare supplies. Because of resource shortages and economic concerns, healthcare facilities could further optimize assets by developing coordinated stockpiles with other local facilities.[1]

HHS/CDC has medical supplies and medications stored in the Strategic National Stockpile (SNS) (http://www.bt.cdc.gov/stockpile). Pandemic and disaster planning should include working with state and federal resources to address access to this supply.

Pandemic Influenza Vaccine

In the event of a pandemic, it is currently estimated that production of initial doses of a vaccine against a novel strain of influenza would take approximately 4 to 6 months. Influenza vaccines are typically grown in fertilized chicken eggs, a process that takes several months. Federal funding has been made available for the development of cell-based vaccine technologies that have the potential to expedite the production of a novel influenza vaccine. In May 2006, HHS awarded contracts totaling more than $1 billion for development of cell-based vaccine technologies.[1, 31, 32]

Pandemic planning should include protocol development and the stockpiling of supplies for administering pandemic influenza vaccine.

Distribution and vaccination recommendations will be coordinated through state and local public health departments. It is critical that healthcare services coordinate with these agencies in order to obtain and administer pandemic vaccine.[1, 32] HHS will determine pandemic vaccine recommendations and prioritization groups (e.g., number of doses recommended, indications, contraindications and ranking of various groups for priority for immunization). Current recommendations regarding pandemic influenza vaccine are available in Part I. Appendix D and in Part II. Supplement 6 of the HHS *Pandemic Influenza Plan* at http://www.hhs.gov/pandemicflu/plan/appendixd.html and http://www.hhs.gov/pandemicflu/plan/sup6.html. Prioritization, based on HHS recommendations, may change. Planning activities should include a process for obtaining and integrating up-to-date pandemic vaccination recommendations.

A vaccine against a pandemic influenza strain may require two doses to provide adequate immunity, therefore, pandemic planning should include developing a procedure to register, track and contact individuals who have received immunizations.[18, 32, 33] Research is currently being conducted into the development of more immunogenic vaccines. Vaccines which contain chemical additives called adjuvants can increase the immune response and require the use of less viral protein which could extend the vaccine supply. Research into other methods of developing vaccines or vaccine delivery systems is ongoing, but as of October 2006, none have received an FDA license.[18, 32, 33]

An important part of pandemic planning is institution of an effective, seasonal influenza campaign which includes encouraging healthcare workers to get vaccinated for seasonal influenza. Unfortunately, current rates of healthcare worker influenza vaccination are not encouraging; only about 40 percent of healthcare workers were vaccinated in 2003.[34]

Antiviral Medication

In contrast to the vaccine, antiviral medications for the treatment of influenza do not need to be specific to the circulating pandemic strain and, thus, are more amenable to stockpiling. There are two classes of antiviral drugs that are U.S. Food and Drug Administration-approved for the treatment of influenza: the neuraminidase inhibitors (oseltamivir and zanamivir) and the M2 inhibitors (adamantine and rimantadine). Unfortunately, influenza A viruses can develop resistance to either class of antiviral drug, and especially rapid emergence of transmissible resistant virus has been reported after treatment with adamantanes.[33, 35, 36] Although hospitals are encouraged to stockpile these drugs, it is impossible to predict which medication will appropriately treat the pandemic virus or if the pandemic virus will develop resistance to one or both classes of medications. Resistance to amantadine and rimantadine has already occurred in the H3N2 seasonal influenza A viruses. As of July 2006, the HHS recommendation for treatment of H5N1 avian and seasonal influenza is to use the medication oseltamivir.[35, 36] Because of worldwide demand, healthcare facilities may have difficulty stockpiling this medication.

The federal government is building a national stockpile with a long-term plan to acquire enough antiviral medications to treat approximately 25 percent of the U.S. population. As of March 2006, there were approximately 5.5 million treatment regimens of antiviral medication in the SNS and approximately 14 million more were on order. The SNS contains both classes of antiviral drugs, but the largest stockpiled medication will be the neuraminidase inhibitor oseltamivir. The targeted SNS level is 50 million courses by 2008. The federal government also plans to subsidize the states' purchase of an additional 31 million courses.[29] State allocations from the national stockpile can be found at http://www.pandemicflu.gov/plan/states/antivirals.html.

The decision to deploy federal assets from the SNS will be made by HHS officials. Each state and federal agency will need a designated representative to make emergency requests and coordinate with HHS to access SNS resources. These representatives will provide logistic guidance on receipt and distribution of the requested assets. Healthcare facilities should integrate and communicate with state planners or there could be difficulty accessing critical medications.[1, 37]

Healthcare plans should be developed for the allocation of antiviral medication with the assumption of limited supplies. Strategies for treatment will be outlined by HHS. Recommendations for use of antivirals may be updated throughout the course of an influenza pandemic based on epidemiologic and laboratory data. Pandemic influenza plans should incorporate the ability to update and adapt to the latest HHS guidance. Planning must include methods to screen patients and employees and to ensure that these medications are administered in a fair manner consistent with HHS recommendations.[37, 38, 39]

A local plan for distribution, point-of-care locations and establishment of priority groups is crucial. Because of the resource limitations and time constraints for efficacy of the medication, developing plans and infrastructure to access, deliver, and prioritize use of this medication must be done in advance. As with vaccinations, this process should be transparent and healthcare facilities should develop a risk communication plan that will keep both healthcare workers and the community updated on current treatment recommendations.[37, 38, 39]

Stockpiles of antiviral medication may be a security issue if there is large pandemic. Consider not only working with hospital security, but also with local and state law enforcement officials to ensure adequate security during a crisis.

Healthcare facilities should also consider stockpiling additional medications to treat secondary infections and pneumonia. Antibiotics and pulmonary medications such as inhalers and nebulizers are stockpile options for treatment and care. Hospitals should arrange for occupational or employee health clinics to develop distribution plans that address employee illness and exposure. These plans need to be flexible to accommodate HHS guidance for distribution and prioritization when a pandemic virus emerges. Once developed, the policy for using stockpiled supplies and administration of antiviral medications should be transparent to employees and the community, including the rationale and justification for the policies.

2005 HHS recommendations for antiviral medical priority groups can be located in Appendix D of the HHS *Pandemic Influenza Plan* at http://www.hhs.gov/pandemicflu/plan/sup7.html.

Personal Protective Equipment
Given that pandemic influenza vaccine will likely not be available until 4 to 6 months into the pandemic and that shortages of antiviral medications are anticipated, PPE will be especially important for protecting healthcare workers. However, logistic and economic considerations may impact the ability for healthcare facilities to stockpile PPE. For example, the SARS outbreak in Toronto lasted approximately 6-7 months. One large hospital reported that at the height of the epidemic the daily consumption of PPE equipment included 3,000 disposable gowns, 14,000 pairs of gloves, 18,000 N95 respirators, 9,500 ear loop masks, and 500 pairs of goggles. In the first week of the SARS outbreak, the hospital purchased $1 million worth of supplies, although their annual hospital budget was only $50 million per year.[9, 40] There were 438 confirmed or suspected SARS cases in Canada.[8] In total, it is esti-

mated that the cost to Ontario province's healthcare system for the SARS outbreak in Toronto was approximately $763 million.[40, 41]

The impact of pandemic influenza would be much greater than the impact of SARS. HHS/CDC modeled a pandemic influenza crisis in the metro Atlanta area with a 25 percent gross attack rate. The model estimated that there would be 412 hospital admissions a day, with a total of 2,013 cases hospitalized in one week during the peak of the outbreak.[42] This is about 4.5 times the number of patients hospitalized during the Toronto SARS outbreak. Although only a model, this example illustrates how complicated the issue of stockpiles and resources will be during a pandemic. Storage of a large supply of PPE may be difficult and costly. Some hospitals are working with distributors to have a stockpile maintained at distributor sites. If there is careful planning for access, transport and delivery of the required PPE, this could be an acceptable option.[4]

HHS suggests stockpiling the following PPE resources:[4]

- Disposable N95 respirators, surgical masks
- Face shields (disposable or reusable)
- Gowns
- Gloves

Influenza A (H5N1): WHO Interim Infection Control Guidelines for Healthcare Facilities, Annex 10 (http://www.who.int/csr/disease/avian_influenza/guidelinestopics/en/index3.html) contains additional consumable resource recommendations.

Outpatient Services and Clinics
HHS/CDC estimates that in a pandemic, approximately 45 million people with pandemic influenza will seek outpatient medical care in the United States (http://www.pandemicflu.gov/plan/pandplan.html). Outpatient clinics should prepare for a surge in utilization of services for pandemic-related illness while continuing to provide medical services for treatment of other acute and chronic medical conditions. Clinics and urgent care centers must identify which services can be curtailed in a pandemic and which services will need to expand. Optimally, clinics should coordinate planning efforts with local hospitals, healthcare organizations and public health agencies. Outpatient clinics could serve as resources to augment healthcare facilities or alternatively, be utilized to reduce the impact on hospitals by treating and addressing care for pandemic patients not requiring hospitalization. Clinics should identify essential personnel and services, identify

critical supplies and prepare for expanded services.[4] Further guidance and information can be found at http://www.pandemicflu.gov/plan/medical.html.

Outpatient service providers should prepare for staffing shortages and develop contingency operations plans. Additionally, protocols for triage and education of patients should be developed. In preparing for an influenza pandemic, HHS recommends that clinics stockpile at least one week of consumable supplies, including PPE, when there is evidence that a pandemic has begun in the United States. Performing triage, ensuring social distancing and isolation of potentially infectious patients will be a challenge in the outpatient care community. Pandemic phone hotlines and websites can be an option to provide education and self-care for clinic patients in order to avoid unnecessary clinic visits. Isolation of potentially ill patients could be difficult; clinics will need protocols and procedures to maintain appropriate distancing and provide education to patients on infection control.[43]

In addition to providing care for patients, clinics have the responsibility for ensuring that employees and healthcare workers are adequately protected during an influenza pandemic. Many of these recommendations in this document can be tailored to the outpatient setting, including these use of appropriate PPE. Clinics may need to develop respiratory protection programs and develop appropriate infection control training for employees. Integration with other clinics and healthcare facilities and public health agencies may assist clinics in this process.

Alternate Care Sites

Alternate care sites may be developed at federal or state discretion to ease the burden of care on healthcare facilities. Some alternate care sites may support the community by providing triage and teaching self-care to individuals who are not critically ill. Vaccination and medication distribution centers may also be opened depending on the availability of these resources.[1, 4] The use and deployment of these facilities will vary, but the requirement to provide a safe workplace does not diminish.

It is important that local and state plans address these alternate sites and determine adequate training and PPE for employees assigned to these facilities. Respiratory protection programs and infection control programs will need to be developed and implemented before the facilities are opened to the public. Healthcare facilities should consider how they can facilitate the provision of training and safety resources to the community before a pandemic situation arises. Primary care providers who have clinics in the community will need to be trained in the use of PPE and infection control practices. HHS has developed a checklist to help clinics develop pandemic disaster plans (http://www.pandemicflu.gov/plan/medical.html).[4] Local and state pandemic planning should include outreach programs to provide necessary training to these healthcare workers. JCAHO has guidance for the development of surge hospitals at http://www.jointcommission.org/PublicPolicy/surge_hospitals.htm.

References

[1] HSC. 2006. National Strategy for Pandemic Influenza Implementation Plan, Homeland Security Council Chapter 6, May.

[2] Zinkovich L., D. Malvey, et al. 2005. Bioterror events: preemptive strategies for healthcare executives. Hosp Top, 83(3):9-15.

[3] Gensheimer, K., M. Meltzer, et al. 2003. Influenza pandemic preparedness. Emerg Infect Dis 9(12): 1645-1648. December.

[4] HHS. 2005. Pandemic Influenza Plan, Supplement 3, Healthcare Planning. U.S. Department of Health and Human Services. 2005.

[5] OSHA. Best practices for hospital-based first receivers of victims from mass casualty incidents involving the release of hazardous substances. OSHA January 2005.

[6] JCAHO. 2006. Joint Commission on Accreditation of Healthcare Organizations, 2006 Hospital Accreditation Standards for Emergency Management Planning, Emergency Management Drills, Infection Control, Disaster Privileges. Last accessed January 18, 2007: http://www.jointcommission.org/NR/rdonlyres/F42AF828-7248-48C0-B4E6-BA18E719A87C/0/06_hap_accred_stds.pdf?HTTP___JCSEARCH.JCAHO.ORG_CGI_BIN_MSMFIND.EXE?RESMASK=MssResEN%2Emskhttp%3A%2F%2Fjcsearch%2Ejcaho%2Eorg%2Fcgi%2Dbin%2FMsmFind%2Eexe%3Fhttp%3A%2F%2Fjcsearch%2Ejcaho%2Eorg%2Fcgi%2Dbin%2FMsmFind%2Eexe%3FRESMASK%3DMssResEN%2Emsk.

[7] Niska R., C. Burt. 2005. Bioterrorism and mass casualty preparedness in hospitals: United States, 2003. National Center for Health Statistics, Hyattsville, MD. Adv Data, no. 364.

[8] Naylor D., S. Basrur, et al. 2003 Learning from SARS: A Report of the National Advisory Committee on SARS and public health: 154-154. October.

[9] Loutfy M., T. Wallington, et al. 2004. Hospital preparedness and SARS. Emerg Infect Dis 10(5): 771-781. May.

[10] Hawryluck L., S. Lapindky, T. Steward. 2005. Clinical review: SARS – lessons in disaster management. Crit Care 9(4): 384-389. August.

[11] HHS. 2005. Pandemic Influenza Plan, Supplement 11, Workforce Support: Psychological Considerations and Information Needs. U.S. Department of Health and Human Services. November.

[12] Johnson M., E. Bone, G. Predy. 2005. Taking care of the sick and scared. Can J Public Health 96(6): 412-414. November-December.

[13] Booth C., T. Stewart. 2005. Severe acute respiratory syndrome and critical care medicine: The Toronto experience. Crit Care Med 33(1) (suppl.): S53-S60.

[14] Booth C., T. Stewart. 2003. Communication in the Toronto critical care community: important lessons learned during SARS. Crit Care 7(6): 405-406. December.

[15] HHS. 2005. Pandemic Influenza Plan, Supplement 8, Disease Control and Prevention. U.S. Department of Health and Human Services. November.

[16] U.S. Department of State. United States Pursues Criminal Charges in Bird Flu Drug Fraud. http://usinfo.state.gov/gi/Archive/2006/Jan/23-183730.html 23 January 2006. Last accessed January 18, 2007.

[17] HHS. 2005. Pandemic Influenza Plan, Supplement 1, Pandemic Influenza Surveillance. U.S. Department of Health and Human Services. November.

[18] Gibbs W., C. Soares. 2005. Preparing for a pandemic. Sci Am. 45-54. November.

[19] McDonald L.C., Simor A.E., et al. 2004 SARS in Healthcare Facilities, Toronto and Tiwan. Emerg Infect Dis. 10(5): 777-781. May.

[20] Maunder R., J. Hunter, et al. 2003. The Immediate psychological and occupational impact of the 2003 SARS outbreak in a teaching hospital. Can Med Assoc J. 168(10): 1245-1251. May.

[21] Ovadia K., I. Gazit, et al. 2005. Better late than never: a re-examination of ethical dilemmas in coping with severe acute respiratory syndrome. J Hosp Infect 61: 75-79.

[22] Reissman D., P. Watson, et al. 2006. Pandemic influenza preparedness: adaptive responses to an evolving challenge. Journal of Homeland Security and Emergency Management, 3(2):1-26.

[23] CSTS. Mental Health and Behavioral Guidelines for Response to Pandemic Influenza. http://www.usuhs.mil/psy/CSTSPandemicAvianInfluenza.pdf. Last accessed January 18, 2007.

[24] U.S. Department of Veterans Affairs. Psychological First Aid Manual. http://www.ncptsd.va.gov/pfa/PFA.html. Last accessed January 18, 2007.

[25] Rambaldini G., W. Kumanan, et al. 2005. The impact of Severe Acute Respiratory Syndrome on medical house staff. J. Gen Intern Med 20:318-385.

[26] Chen C.S., H.Y. Wu., et al. 2005. Psychological distress of nurses in Taiwan who worked during the outbreak of SARS. Psychiatr Serv 56(1): 76-9.

[27] HHS. 2005. Pandemic Influenza Plan, Supplement 4, Infection Control. U.S. Department of Health and Human Services. November.

[28] Higgins W., C. Wainright, et al. 2004. Assessing hospital preparedness using an instrument based on the Mass Casualty Disaster Plan Checklist: Results of a statewide survey. Am J Infect Control 32(6): 327-332.

[29] HHS. 2006. Pandemic Planning Update A Report from Secretary Michael O. Leavitt. Department of Health and Human Services. March 13.

[30] JCAHO. 2003. Health Care at the Crossroads: strategies for creating and sustaining community-wide emergency preparedness systems. Joint Commission on Accreditation of Healthcare Organizations.

[31] News Release. May 4, 2006 HHS Awards Contracts Totaling More than $1 Billion to Develop Cell-Based Influenza Vaccine. http://www.hhs.gov/news/press/2006pres/20060504.html. Last accessed January 18, 2007.

[32] HHS. 2005. Pandemic Influenza Plan, Supplement 6, Vaccine Distribution and Use. U.S. Department of Health and Human Services. November.

[33] Monto A., Vaccine and Antiviral Drugs in Pandemic Preparedness. Emerg Infect Dis. 12(1); 55-60. January.

[34] MMWR. 2005. Interventions to increase influenza vaccination of health-care workers – California and Minnesota. Morbidity and Mortality Weekly. 54(08): 196-199. March 4.

[35] CDC. 2006. CDC Recommends against the use of amantadine and rimantadine for the treatment or prophylaxis of influenza in the United States during the 2005-06 influenza season. CDC Health Alert, Centers for Disease Control and Prevention. Last

accessed January 18, 2007: http://www.cdc.gov/flu/han011406.htm.

[36] WHO. 2006. Avian Influenza, including Influenza A (H5N1), in Humans: WHO Interim Infection Control Guideline for Health Care Facilities. World Health Organization. February 9. Last accessed on January 18, 2007 at http://www.who.int/csr/disease/avian_influenza/guidelines/infectioncontrol1/en/.

[37] HHS. 2005. Pandemic Influenza Plan, Supplement 7, Antiviral Drug Distribution and Use. U.S. Department of Health and Human Services. November.

[38] Cinti S. 2005. Pandemic influenza: are we ready? Disaster Manag Response 3:61067.

[39] Cinti S., C. Chenoweth, A. Monto. 2005. Preparing for Pandemic Influenza: should hospitals stockpile oseltamivir? Infect Control Hosp Epidemiol 26(11); 852-854. November.

[40] Friesen S. 2003. The impact of SARS on health-care supply chains. Logistics Quarterly 9(2). Last accessed March 28, 2006: www.lq.ca/issues/fall2003/articles/article01.html.

[41] Osterholm M. 2005. Preparing for the next pandemic. Foreign Aff. July/August. Last accessed June 30, 2006: http://www.foreignaffairs.org/20050701faessay84402/michael-t-osterholm/preparing-for-the-next-pandemic.html.

[42] FluSurge 2.0 Manual. Last accessed June 30, 2006: http://www.cdc.gov/flu/pdf/FluSurge2.0_Manual_060705.pdf.

[43] Medical offices and clinics pandemic influenza preparedness checklist. Last accessed August 3, 2006 http://www.pandemicflu.gov/plan/medical.html.

OSHA Standards of Special Importance

The role of OSHA is "to assure safe and healthful working conditions for working men and women."[1] Employers have a responsibility to furnish employees "a place of employment which is free from recognized hazards that are causing or are likely to cause death or serious physical harm."[1] In addition, employers must comply with occupational safety and health standards promulgated by OSHA or by a state with an OSHA-approved state plan. (More information about state occupational safety and health programs can be found at http://www.osha.gov/fso/osp/index.html.) OSHA standards applicable to healthcare facilities are addressed in the standards for General Industry. In addition, the Respiratory Protection standard, the Personal Protective Equipment standard, and the Bloodborne Pathogens standard have special importance to pandemic preparedness and response.

Respiratory Protection Standard - 29 CFR 1910.134

The primary objective of OSHA's Respiratory Protection standard is to protect employees against inhalation of harmful airborne substances or oxygen-deficient air. This standard applies to all occupational airborne exposures where employees are exposed to a hazardous level of an airborne contaminant. The inhalation of pathogenic organisms known to cause human disease is covered by this standard.

Employers are required to use feasible engineering controls as the primary means of controlling air contaminants. Respirators should be used for protection only when engineering controls have been shown to be technologically or economically infeasible or while they are being instituted for the control of the hazard.

Healthcare facilities requiring the use of respirators must implement a comprehensive respiratory protection program. These programs are to be overseen by a qualified program administrator and have key elements that include respirator selection, training, medical certification, fit testing, maintenance and cleaning, and program review.

Additional information on the Respiratory Protection standard is included in Appendix C in this document. Information describing all of the elements of a comprehensive respiratory protection program and the use of respirators can be found at http://www.osha.gov/SLTC/respiratoryprotection/index.html.

Personal Protective Equipment Standard - 29 CFR 1910.132

When engineering controls, work practices, and administrative controls are infeasible or do not provide sufficient protection, employers must provide appropriate personal protective equipment (PPE) and ensure its proper use. PPE is worn to minimize exposure to a variety of workplace hazards. PPE can include protection for eyes, face, head, and extremities. Gowns, face shields, gloves, and respirators are examples of commonly used PPE within healthcare facilities.

Employers must conduct a workplace hazard assessment to determine if hazards are present that necessitate the use of PPE. The employer must verify that the required workplace hazard assessment has been performed through a written certification that identifies the workplace evaluated; the person certifying that the evaluation has been performed; the date(s) of the hazard assessment; and, which identifies the document as a certification of hazard assessment. Based on the hazard assessment, employers are to select PPE that will protect employees from the identified hazards. Employees are to receive training to ensure that they understand the hazards present, the necessity of the PPE, and its limitations. In addition, they must learn how to properly put on, take off, adjust, and wear PPE. Finally, employees must understand the proper care, maintenance, and disposal of PPE.

Healthcare employers can receive more information about the Personal Protective Equipment standard at http://www.osha.gov/SLTC/personalprotectiveequipment/index.html.

Bloodborne Pathogens Standard - 29 CFR 1910.1030

OSHA's Bloodborne Pathogens standard is a regulation that protects employees against health hazards related to the occupational exposure to bloodborne pathogens. The standard applies to any employee who is occupationally exposed to human blood or certain other potentially infectious materials (e.g., pleural fluid, any body fluids visibly contaminated with blood, any unfixed human tissue or organ). The Bloodborne Pathogens standard has provisions requiring exposure control plans, engineering and work practice controls, PPE, hepatitis B vaccination, hazard communication, training, and recordkeeping.

Additional information on the Bloodborne Pathogens standard is available at http://www.osha.gov/SLTC/bloodbornepathogen/index.html.

General Duty Clause

In addition to compliance with the hazard-specific safety and health standards, employers must provide their employees with a workplace free from recognized hazards likely to cause death or serious physical harm. Employers can be cited for violating the General Duty Clause of the OSH Act if they do not take reasonable steps to abate or address such recognized hazards.[2]

References

[1] OSHA. Occupational Safety and Health Act of 1970 (OSH Act).

[2] 29 U.S.C. 654(a)(1).

Appendix A
Pandemic Influenza Internet Resources

General Pandemic Planning Resources		
Department of Health and Human Services	http://www.pandemicflu.gov	Federal/State pandemic disaster planning resources; updated as new information becomes available.
Department of Health and Human Services	http://www.pandemicflu.gov/plan/tab6.html	Checklists for specific healthcare services, hospitals, clinics, home health, long-term care, EMS.
Centers for Disease Control and Prevention	http://www2a.cdc.gov/od/fluaid	The FluAid program is a resource for state and local planners to estimate range of deaths, hospitalizations, and outpatient visits for a community.
	http://www.cdc.gov/flu/flusurge.htm	The FluSurge program estimates the impact of a pandemic on the surge capacity of individual healthcare facilities, (i.e., hospital beds, ventilators).
Agency for Healthcare Research and Quality	Multiple resources on disaster planning including surge capacity, stockpiles, and developing alternate care sites:	
	http://www.ahrq.gov/browse/bioterbr.htm	AHRQ disaster planning website
	http://www.ahrq.gov/research/havbed/	Issues addressing bed capacity
	http://www.ahrq.gov/research/shuttered/shuttools.pdf	Opening shuttered hospitals to address surge capacity
	http://www.ahrq.gov/news/ulp/btbriefs/btbrief3.htm	Conferences to optimize surge capacity
	http://www.ahrq.gov/research/devmodels/	Development of models for emergency preparedness
	http://www.ahrq.gov/research/epri/	Emergency preparedness resource inventory
	http://www.ahrq.gov/research/altstand/	Altered standards of care in mass casualty event
	http://www.ahrq.gov/research/altsites.htm	Alternate site use during an emergency
	http://www.ahrq.gov/research/biomodel.htm	Computer staffing model
	http://www.ahrq.gov/research/health/	Integrating with public health agencies
	http://www.ahrq.gov/research/biomodel3/toc.asp#top	Bioterrorism and Epidemic Response Model

Department of Veterans Affairs	http://www.publichealth.va.gov/flu/pan-demicflu.htm	The VA has information on infection control and other pandemic resources.
World Health Organization	http://www.who.int/csr/resources/publications/influenza/WHO_CDS_CSR_GIP_2005_5/en/index.html http://www.who.int/csr/en/	International planning strategies and global pandemic information
Food and Drug Administration	http://www.fda.gov/oc/opacom/hottopics/flu.html	Information on vaccine, antiviral medication, fraud investigations.

Resources for Coordination with State and Local Agencies

Association of State and Territorial Health Officials	http://www.astho.org/	Resources for pandemic planning, including state health department listings and state pandemic plans.
California	http://www.heics.com/	Hospital Emergency Incident Command System (HEICS), an example of an emergency manage-ment plan for healthcare facilities.
Joint Commission on Accreditation of Healthcare Organizations	http://www.jointcommission.org/PublicPolicy/ep_guide.htm http://www.jointcommission.org/PublicPolicy/surge_hospitals.htm	Resources for integrations with community disaster planning. Surge hospital planning and implementation.

Resources for Medications and Vaccination Information and Planning

Agency for Healthcare Research and Quality	http://www.ahrq.gov/research/biomodel3/	Part of the Weil/Cornell Bioterrorism and Epidemic Response Module (BERM), specifically addressing planning for mass prophylaxis.
Department of Health and Human Services	http://www.pandemicflu.gov/vaccine	Up-to-date information on vaccines, medication and tests for pandemic influenza.

Disaster and Pandemic Influenza Tabletop Exercises and Drills

Department of Health and Human Services	http://www.hhs.gov/nvpo/pandemics/tabletopex.html	Tools to assist planning and conduct-ing tabletop exercises for pandemic influenza planning.

Appendix B
Infection Control Communication Tools
for Healthcare Workers

1. **Hand Hygiene, Centers for Disease Control and Prevention:**
   MMWR Recommendations and Reports October 25, 2002/51(RR16); 1-44.
   Guideline for Hand Hygiene in Healthcare Settings
   http://www.cdc.gov/mmwr/preview/mmwrhtml/rr5116a1.htm
   Posters:
   http://www.cdc.gov/mmwr/PDF/rr/rr5116.pdf
   http://www.cdc.gov/od/oc/media/pressrel/fs021025.htm
   http://www.cdc.gov/handhygiene/materials.htm

2. **PPE Donning and Doffing Procedures, Centers for Disease Control and Prevention**
   Posters:
   http://www.cdc.gov/ncidod/sars/pdf/ppeposter1322.pdf
   http://www.cdc.gov/ncidod/sars/pdf/ppeposter148.pdf

3. **Department of Veterans Affairs**
   Posters:
   http://www.publichealth.va.gov/InfectionDontPassItOn/index_hand.htm
   http://www.publichealth.va.gov/InfectionDontPassItOn/index_hand_resp.htm
   http://www.publichealth.va.gov/InfectionDontPassItOn/Index_ppe.htm

4. **Occupational Safety and Health Administration, guidance on the proper use of PPE:**
   http://www.osha.gov/dts/osta/bestpractices/html/hospital_firstreceivers.html

Appendix B-1
Factors Influencing Adherence to Hand Hygiene Practices

Reproduced from MMWR Recommendations and Reports October 25, 2002/51(RR16); 1-44.
Guideline for Hand Hygiene in Healthcare Settings, Box 1.

Observed risk factors for poor adherence to recommended hand hygiene practices
- Physician status (rather than a nurse)
- Nursing assistant status (rather than a nurse)
- Male sex
- Working in an intensive care unit
- Working during the week (versus the weekend)
- Wearing gowns/gloves
- Automated sink
- Activities with high risk of cross-transmission
- High number of opportunities for hand hygiene per hour of patient care

Self-reported factors for poor adherence with hand hygiene
- Handwashing agents cause irritation and dryness
- Sinks are inconveniently located/shortage of sinks
- Lack of soap and paper towels
- Often too busy/insufficient time
- Understaffing/overcrowding
- Patient needs take priority
- Hand hygiene interferes with healthcare worker relationships with patients
- Low risk of acquiring infection from patients
- Wearing of gloves/beliefs that glove use obviates the need for hand hygiene
- Lack of knowledge of guidelines/protocols
- Not thinking about it/forgetfulness
- No role model from colleagues or superiors
- Skepticism regarding the value of hand hygiene
- Disagreement with the recommendations
- Lack of scientific information of definitive impact of improved hand hygiene on healthcare–associated infection rates

Additional perceived barriers to appropriate hand hygiene
- Lack of active participation in hand hygiene promotion at individual or institutional level
- Lack of role model for hand hygiene
- Lack of institutional priority for hand hygiene
- Lack of administrative sanction of noncompliers/rewarding compliers
- Lack of institutional safety climate

Source: Adapted from Pittet D. Improving compliance with hand hygiene in hospitals. Infect Control Hosp Epidemiol 2000;21:381–6.

Appendix B-2
Elements of Healthcare Worker Educational and Motivational Programs
Reproduced from MMWR Recommendations and Reports October 25, 2002/51(RR16); 1-44.
Guideline for Hand Hygiene in Healthcare Settings, Box 2.

Rationale for hand hygiene
- Potential risks of transmission of microorganisms to patients
- Potential risks of healthcare worker colonization or infection caused by organisms acquired from the patient
- Morbidity, mortality, and costs associated with healthcare–associated infections

Indications for hand hygiene
- Contact with a patient's intact skin (e.g., taking a pulse or blood pressure, performing physical examinations, lifting the patient in bed) (25,26,45,48,51,53)*
- Contact with environmental surfaces in the immediate vicinity of patients (46,51,53,54)*
- After glove removal (50,58,71)*

Techniques for hand hygiene
- Amount of hand hygiene solution
- Duration of hand hygiene procedure
- Selection of hand hygiene agents
  - Alcohol-based hand rubs are the most efficacious agents for reducing the number of bacteria on the hands of personnel. Antiseptic soaps and detergents are the next most effective, and non-antimi-crobial soaps are the least effective (1,398).
  - Soap and water are recommended for visibly soiled hands.
  - Alcohol-based hand rubs are recommended for routine decontamination of hands for all clinical indications (except when hands are visibly soiled) and as one of the options for surgical hand hygiene.

Methods to maintain hand skin health
- Lotions and creams can prevent or minimize skin dryness and irritation caused by irritant contact dermatitis
- Acceptable lotions or creams to use
- Recommended schedule for applying lotions or creams

Expectations of patient care managers/administrators
- Written statements regarding the value of, and support for, adherence to recommended hand hygiene practices
- Role models demonstrating adherence to recommended hand hygiene practices (399)*

Indications for, and limitations of, glove use
- Hand contamination may occur as a result of small, undetected holes in examination gloves (321,361)*
- Contamination may occur during glove removal (50)*
- Wearing gloves does not replace the need for hand hygiene (58)*
- Failure to remove gloves after caring for a patient may lead to transmission of microorganizations from one patient to another (373)*

*The numbers in parentheses after some of the elements refer to references in the original MMWR document.

Appendix B-3
Strategies for Successful Promotion of Hand Hygiene in Hospitals

Adapted from MMWR Recommendations and Reports October 25, 2002/51(RR16); 1-44. Guideline for Hand Hygiene in Healthcare Settings, Table 9. Strategies for Successful Promotion of Hand Hygiene in Hospitals.

Strategies for Successful Promotion of Hand Hygiene in Hospitals
- Education
- Routine observation and feedback
- Engineering control
  ◦ Make hand hygiene possible, easy, and convenient
  ◦ Make alcohol-based hand rub available (at least in high demand situations)
- Patient education
- Reminders in the workplace
- Administrative sanction/rewarding
- Change in hand hygiene agent
- Promote/facilitate skin care for healthcare workers' hands
- Obtain active participation at individual and institutional level
- Improve institutional safety climate
- Enhance individual and institutional self-efficacy
- Avoid overcrowding, understaffing, and excessive workload
- Combine several of above strategies

Appendix B-4
Pandemic Influenza Precautions for Veterans Administration Healthcare Facility Staff

Reproduced with permission from the Department of Veterans Affairs Pandemic Plan, Appendix E-2: Chart of Pandemic Influenza Precautions for VA Healthcare Facility Staff.

Airborne Infection Isolation and Contact Precautions, in addition to Standard Precautions

This combination of precautions offers the best protection for health care facility staff, especially at the onset of a pandemic before transmission patterns are well understood.

	Hand cleaning	Gloves	Gowns	Eye protection	Respiratory protection	Room
Airborne Infection Isolation + Contact	• Between patients • Immediately after glove removal • Whenever hands may be contaminated by secretions or body fluids • Use an alcohol-based hand rub or wash with antimicrobial soap and water	• When caring for patients • When touching areas or handling items contaminated by patients	• With patient contact	• When within 3 feet of patient • With aerosol-generating procedures	• Use fit-tested N95 mask OR positive air purifying respirator (PAPR) or fit-tested elastomeric respirator Patients • Wear masks during transport. • Use masks with elastic straps; avoid masks that tie on.	• Negative air-flow private room when possible • Air exhausted outdoors or through high-efficiency filtration. • Door kept closed.

Droplet Precautions, in addition to Standard Precautions

This combination of precautions should be used if droplet transmission appears to be the common mode of transmission or when incapable of using Airborne Infection Isolation and Contact Precautions.

	Hand cleaning	Gloves	Gowns	Eye protection	Respiratory protection	Room
Droplet	• Between patients • Immediately after glove removal • Whenever hands may be contaminated by secretions or body fluids • Use an alcohol-based hand rub or wash with antimicrobial soap and water	• When caring for patients • When touching areas or handling items contaminated by patients	• Not required	• With aerosol-generating procedures	• Wear surgical or procedure-type masks in patient rooms or when within 3 feet of patients; change when moist • Wear fit-tested N95 respirator or equivalent with aerosol generating procedures Patients • Wear masks during transport. • Use masks with elastic straps; avoid masks that tie on.	• Private room when possible • Door may be open.

Appendix B-5
Public Health Measures Against Pandemic Influenza for Individuals, Healthcare Providers, and Organizations

Reproduced with permission from Department of Veterans Affairs Pandemic Plan, Appendix E-3: Chart of Public Health Measures Against Pandemic Influenza Precautions for Individuals, Health Care Providers, and Organizations.

The measures in the chart below may be important to reduce transmission of pandemic influenza in VA facilities and other settings.

Who Can Act?	What Public Health Measures?	Why?
Individuals	Cleaning hands regularly.	Reduces transfer of microorganisms from the hands to the eyes, nose, or mouth. Reduces transmission of microorganisms carried on hands from person to person.
	Following respiratory hygiene rules (covering the mouth and nose with tissues when coughing or sneezing).	Prevents dispersal of respiratory viruses in the air.
	Getting seasonal influenza vaccinations.	Prevents individuals from getting/transmitting seasonal influenza, which reduces burden on health care system, and keeps the individual well and able to conduct daily business. Reduces likelihood of genetic reassortment of influenza strains when a person is infected with more than one strain. Helps people become accustomed to getting vaccinations.
	Avoiding contact with sick persons—staying at least three to five feet away.	Reduces likelihood of one's getting and transmitting influenza.
	Staying home when sick—from work, school, public places.	Reduces transmission of influenza to other persons.
	Wearing masks when sick with influenza, if able to tolerate.	Reduces transmission to others.

Who Can Act?	What Public Health Measures?	Why?
Health care providers	Tracing contacts.	Locates and allows potentially exposed persons to be informed and able to take measures to avoid exposing others.
	Isolating people with suspected or confirmed influenza.	Reduces transmission of influenza to others.
	Quarantining people exposed to influenza.	Reduces transmission of influenza to other persons. Because the incubation period of influenza is about 2 days, quarantine time would also be short (actual time will be determined by the characteristics of the pandemic influenza virus).
	Wearing personal protective equipment—masks or respirators, gowns, gloves, goggles.	Reduces risk of getting influenza and potential of transmitting it to others.
Business, community, regional, and national organizations and leaders	Developing, manufacturing, stockpiling, and distributing antiviral medications.	Treats influenza or prevents its spread.
	Developing, manufacturing, stockpiling, and distributing vaccine.	Prevents influenza.
	Reducing non-essential travel.	Reduces the number of persons an individual has contact with and slows the spread of influenza from region to region.
	Closing schools.	Children usually have many more close contacts than adults; closing schools greatly reduces transmission of influenza within schools, within families, and within communities.
	Declaring "snow days" (temporarily closing businesses, offices), postponing public gatherings.	Reduces contacts among persons; has potential to reduce transmission.
	Enabling employees to work from home; making teleworking/telecommuting possible.	Reduces contacts among persons; has potential to reduce transmission.
	Partitioning space.	Limiting access to a building or facility by screening those who enter for fever, respiratory symptoms, and possible recent exposure.

Appendix C
Implementation and Planning for Respiratory Protection Programs in Healthcare Settings

Appendix C-1
Respiratory Protection Programs

OSHA Respiratory Protection Standard

The OSHA Respiratory Protection standard (29 CFR 1910.134) requires employers to establish and maintain a respiratory protection program to protect their respirator-wearing employees. Employers must provide respirators when such equipment is necessary to protect the health of employees. The respirator provided must be suitable for its intended purpose. When an employer is required to provide respirators, the employer must establish and maintain a respiratory protection program.

Respiratory Protection Program

A respiratory protection program is a cohesive collection of worksite-specific procedures and policies that addresses all respiratory protection elements required by the standard. For example, a respiratory protection program must contain specific procedures describing how respirators will be selected, fitted, used, maintained and inspected in a particular workplace. A written program is needed because health and safety programs can be more effectively implemented and evaluated if the procedures are available in a written form for study and review.

Also, a written respiratory protection program is the best way to ensure that the unique characteristics of the worksite are taken into account. Developing the written program encourages the employer to thoroughly assess and document information pertaining to the respiratory hazards to which their employees will potentially be exposed, both during normal operating conditions and during reasonably foreseeable emergencies.

A respiratory protection program is required to include the following elements (as applicable):

- Procedures for selecting appropriate respirators for use in the workplace.
- Fit testing tight-fitting respirators.
- Cleaning, disinfecting, storing, inspecting, repairing, removing from service or discarding, and otherwise maintaining respirators. Also, you must establish schedules for these elements.
- Ensuring adequate air supply, quantity, and flow of breathing air for atmosphere supplying respirators.

- Provisions for medical evaluation of employees who must use respirators.
- Training employees in the proper use of respirators (including putting them on and removing them), the limitations on their use, and their maintenance.
- Regularly evaluating the effectiveness of the program.

Respiratory Protection Program Administrator

The employer must designate a program administrator to run the program and evaluate its effectiveness. An individual is qualified to be a program administrator if he or she has appropriate training or experience in accord with the program's level of complexity. This training or experience is appropriate if it enables the program administrator to fulfill the minimum standard requirements of recognizing, evaluating, and controlling the hazards in the workplace. For example, if the program requires air-supplying respirators for use in immediately dangerous to life or health environments, the program administrator must have training and experience pertaining to the use of this type of equipment. Similarly, if air-supplying respirators are not used and there are no significant respiratory hazards at the workplace, someone with less sophisticated experience or training might be able to effectively serve in this position.

Ultimately, the appropriate qualifications for the respiratory protection program administrator must be determined based on the particular respiratory hazards that exist, or that are reasonably anticipated, at the workplace.

Medical Evaluations

Employers must medically evaluate their employees' ability to wear a respirator. Medical evaluations are required for both positive pressure and negative pressure respirators. Medical evaluation can be performed by using a medical questionnaire or by performing an initial medical examination that obtains the same information as the medical questionnaire. Employers must allow the employee to be evaluated during the employee's normal working hours or at a time that is convenient to the employee, and employers are responsible for paying for this service (even if the employee has coverage under an insurance plan).

Employers must identify a physician or another licensed healthcare professional (PLHCP) to perform the medical evaluations. Physicians are not the only healthcare professionals allowed to perform medical evaluations for respirator use. The Respiratory Protection standard allows any PLHCP to administer the medical questionnaire (described below) or to conduct the medical examination if doing so is within the scope of the PLHCP's license. Employers may check with PLHCPs in their local area to see if performing the medical evaluation is within the scope of their professional license, or employers may check with the state's licensing board.

The Medical Questionnaire

The medical questionnaire is designed to identify general medical conditions that place employees who use respirators at risk of serious medical consequences. If employers choose to use the medical questionnaire to conduct the medical evaluation, they must use the questionnaire contained in the Respiratory Protection standard (Appendix C of the standard, Part A., Sections 1 and 2). The PLHCP determines whether or not Part B of the questionnaire needs to be administered, and the PLHCP can alter the questions in Part B in any manner he or she thinks is appropriate. Employers may choose to use medical examinations in place of the questionnaire, but they are not required to do so. Medical examinations must be provided for an employee who gives a positive response to any question among questions 1-8 of Part A, Section 2 in Appendix C of the standard. Although the questionnaire does not have to be administered during the medical examination, the PLHCP must obtain the same information from the employee that is contained in the questionnaire.

Fit Testing

The Respiratory Protection standard requires employers to conduct fit testing on all employees who are required to wear a respirator that includes a tight-fitting facepiece. Fit testing is a procedure used to determine how well a respirator "fits"—that is, whether the respirator forms an adequate seal on the user's face. If a good facepiece-to-face seal is not achieved, the respirator will provide a lower level of protection than it was designed to provide. For example, without a good seal, the respirator can allow contaminants to leak into the facepiece and be inhaled by the user.

There are two types of fit testing: quantitative and qualitative. Quantitative fit testing is a method of measuring the amount of leakage into a respirator. It is a numeric assessment of how well a respirator fits a particular individual. To quantitatively fit test a respirator, sampling probes or other measuring devices must be placed to measure aerosol concentrations both outside and on the inside of the respirator facepiece. Qualitative fit testing is a non-numeric pass/fail test that relies on the respirator wearer's response to a substance ("test agent") used in the test to determine respirator fit. In qualitative fit testing, after performing user seal checks, the respirator wearer stands in an enclosure and a test agent is introduced, such as banana oil (isoamyl acetate), saccharin, Bitrex, or irritant smoke (without a test enclosure). If the individual can smell or taste the test agent (or is irritated by the smoke), this indicates that the agent leaked into the facepiece and that the respirator has failed the test because a good facepiece-to-face seal has not been achieved. If the employee cannot successfully complete the qualitative test with a particular respirator, the employee must then be tested with another make, size, or brand of respirator.

Fit testing must be conducted for all employees required to wear tight-fitting facepiece respirators as follows:

- Prior to initial use.
- Whenever an employee switches to a different tight-fitting facepiece respirator (for example, a different size, make, model, or style).
- At least annually.

Employers must ensure that an additional fit test is conducted if an employee experiences a change in physical condition that could affect the seal on the tight-fitting facepiece respirator. This requirement is triggered by a physical change:

- Reported by the respirator user.
- Observed by the employer, a physician or other licensed healthcare professional, the supervisor, or the program administrator.
- Physical changes in the employee that might affect the facepiece-to-face seal could include, for example, an obvious change in body weight, facial scarring, dental work, or cosmetic surgery.

If, after fit testing, an employee reports that his or her respirator does not fit properly, you must allow the employee a reasonable opportunity to select a different tight-fitting facepiece respirator. After another respirator is selected, you must conduct a new fit test on the employee's replacement equipment. An employee might determine that the facepiece does not establish an effective facepiece-to-face seal, for example, upon smelling a worksite contaminant while wearing the respirator with new cartridges. Or an employee might hear or feel air leaking around the facepiece-to-face seal. The employee's determination also can be based on factors unrelated to the particular worksite. For example, the employee might find that he or she cannot wear the respirator for extended periods without experiencing irritation or pain.

Employers must ensure that all fit testing conducted for employees required to wear tight-fitting facepiece respirators follows the OSHA approved protocols. Detailed protocols for qualitative and quantitative fit testing are provided as part of the standard (see Appendices A and B of the standard). These protocols specify that you must have on hand during fit testing all types and sizes of respirators that are available for use at the worksite. This allows you to ensure that each employee is tested with the same type of respirator (make, model, style, and size) that he or she will wear at the worksite.

Tight-Fitting and Loose-fitting Respirator Facepieces
A tight-fitting facepiece is intended to form a complete seal with the respirator wearer's face. This seal must be sufficiently tight to prevent any contaminants in the work environment from leaking around the edges of the facepiece into the user's breathing air.

In contrast, a loose-fitting facepiece is specifically designed to form a partial seal with the user's face. Such a facepiece typically covers at least the head and includes a system through which clean air is distributed into the breathing zone. For example, hoods and helmets are loose-fitting facepieces. Such equipment does not rely on a tight facepiece-to-face seal to protect the wearer, and is useful for employees with facial hair or other physical characteristics that make it difficult to wear a tight-fitting facepiece.

Preventing Leaks in the Facepiece Seal
Facepiece seals and valves are important in tight-fitting respirators. Tight-fitting respirators have a complete seal to the face. If there is a leak in the seal of a tight-fitting respirator or valve, then the respirator cannot reduce the wearer's exposures to respiratory hazards. You must be sure that nothing interferes with the seal of the respirator to the employee's face or with the valves. Conditions that can interfere with the seal or valve include:

- Facial hair

- Facial scars
- Jewelry or headgear
- Missing dentures
- Corrective glasses or goggles or other PPE such as:
  - Face shields
  - Protective clothing
  - Helmets
  - Eyeglass insert or spectacle kits

Employees may use the equipment in the above list with tight-fitting respirators if the employer ensures that the equipment is worn in a way that:

- Does not interfere with the face-to-facepiece seal.
- Does not distort the employee's vision.
- Does not cause physical harm to the employee (e.g., if the eyeglass insert did not fit properly so that the tight fit of the respirator caused the insert to press against his or her forehead, eyes, or temples).

If an employee wears corrective glasses or goggles or other personal protective equipment, the employer shall ensure that such equipment is worn in a manner that does not interfere with the seal of the facepiece to the face of the user.

Conducting User Seal Checks
To conduct a user seal check, the employee performs a negative or positive pressure fit check.

For the negative pressure check, the employee:

- Covers the respirator inlets (cartridges, canisters, or seals)
- Gently inhales, and
- Holds breath for 10 seconds.

The facepiece should collapse on the employee's face and remain collapsed.

For the positive pressure check, the employee:

- Covers the respirator exhalation valve(s); and
- Gently exhales.

The facepiece should hold the positive pressure for a few seconds. During this time, the employee should not hear or feel the air leaking out of the face-to-facepiece seal. Appendix B-1 of the OSHA Respiratory Protection standard provides detailed instructions on how to conduct the user seal check. The manufacturer's recommended procedures for checking the facepiece seal may be used if the employer demonstrates that the manufacturer's procedures are as effective as those described in Appendix B-1 of the OSHA Respiratory Protection standard.

Maintenance and Care of Respirators

Employers must provide respirator users with equipment that is clean, sanitary, and in good working order. To accomplish this, employers must have a system of respirator care and maintenance as a component of their respiratory protection program. Regular care and maintenance is important to ensure that the equipment functions as designed and protects the user from the threat of illness or death.

Your system of respirator care and maintenance must provide for:

- Cleaning and disinfection procedures
- Proper storage
- Regular inspections
- Repair methods

Cleaning and Disinfection

Respirator equipment must be regularly cleaned and disinfected according to specified procedures (see Appendix B-2 of the standard) or according to manufacturer specifications that are of equivalent effectiveness.

Cleaning and disinfection procedures are divided into the following:

- Disassembly of components
- Cleaning and disinfecting
- Rinsing, drying, and reassembly
- Inspection

The frequency of cleaning and disinfecting or sanitizing respirators will depend in part on whether your employees share the equipment or are issued respirators for their exclusive use. Worksite conditions also will dictate cleaning frequency, e.g., working in a dirty environment. In addition, if individual employees are required to clean their own respirators, you must allow time during work hours for users to perform this function.

Proper Storage Procedures for Respirators

Employers must store respirators in a manner that:

- Protects them from contamination, dust, sunlight, extreme temperatures, excessive moisture, damaging chemicals, or other destructive conditions.
- Prevents the facepiece or valves from becoming deformed.
- Follows all storage precautions issued by the respirator manufacturer.

In addition, if a respirator is intended for emergency use, it must be:

- Kept accessible to the work area, but not in an area that may itself become involved in an emergency and become contaminated or inaccessible.
- Stored in a compartment or cover (e.g., on a fire truck) that is clearly identified as containing emergency equipment.

Training and Information

Employee training is a critical part of a successful respiratory protection program and is essential for correct respirator use. Employers must provide training to their employees who are required to wear respirators and must ensure that each employee can demonstrate knowledge of at least the following:

1. **Why the respirator is necessary and how improper fit, usage, and maintenance can make the respirator ineffective.**
   Training must address the identification of hazards, the extent of employee exposure to those hazards, and the potential health effects of exposure. The training that is required under the Hazard Communication standard (29 CFR 1910.1200) can satisfy this requirement for chemical hazards. Employees must understand that proper fit, usage, and maintenance of respirators is critical to ensure that they can perform their protective function.

2. **The limitations and capabilities of the selected respirator.**
   Training must cover how the respirator operates. Included must be an explanation of how the respirator provides protection by filtering the air, absorbing the gas or vapor, or by supplying a clean source of air. Limitations on the use of the equipment, such as prohibitions against using an air-purifying respirator in an immediately dangerous to life and health atmosphere, and why not, must also be explained.

3. **How to inspect, put on and remove, and check the seals of the respirator.**
   Employers must train employees how to recognize problems that may decrease the effectiveness of the respirator and what steps to follow if a problem is detected, such as the person to whom problems should be reported and where replacement equipment can be obtained if needed. If specialized personnel conduct inspections, individual respirator wearers only need to be taught about the portions of the inspection

process that are their responsibility. Training must also cover how to properly put on and remove the respirator to ensure that respirator fit in the workplace is as close as possible to the fit obtained during fit testing.

4. **The proper respirator maintenance and storage procedures.**
The extent of training required may vary according to workplace conditions. If employees are individually responsible for storing and maintaining respirators, detailed training may be necessary. If specialized personnel perform these functions, employees only need to be informed of the maintenance and storage procedures.

5. **The general requirements of the Respiratory Protection standard.**
Employers must ensure that employees are aware, in general, of the employer's obligations under the standard. This discussion need not focus on the standard's provisions but could, for example, simply inform employees that employers are obligated to develop a written program, properly select respirators, evaluate respirator use, correct deficiencies in respirator use, conduct medical evaluations, provide for the maintenance, storage and cleaning of respirators, and retain and provide access to specific records.

Employers must ensure that, before an employee is required to use a respirator in the workplace, he or she understands the information provided and can use the respirator properly. This can be done by reviewing the training with the employee either orally or in writing, and by reviewing the employee's hands-on use of respirators. Training must be conducted in a manner that is understandable to the employees. This means that your program should be tailored to your employees' education level and language background. Employers must provide the required training prior to requiring an employee to use a respirator in the workplace.

If employers can demonstrate that a new employee has received training within the last 12 months and that the new employee has the necessary knowledge, employers are not required to repeat this training. In cases where training in some elements is lacking or inadequate, employers are required to provide training in those elements. Previous training not repeated initially must be provided no later than 12 months from the date of the previous training.

Retraining

Employers must retrain employees in the proper use of respirators annually. They must also retrain employees when:

- Changes in the workplace or the type of respirator make previous training obsolete.
- The knowledge and skill necessary to use the respirator properly has not been retained by the employee.
- Any other situation arises in which retraining appears necessary to ensure safe respirator use.

Appendix C-2
Readiness Plan for Epidemic Respiratory Infection:
A Guideline for Operations for Use by the Dartmouth-Hitchcock Medical Center-
Lebanon Campus and the Dartmouth College Health Service
Reproduced with permission

Readiness Plan for Epidemic Respiratory Infection:
A Guideline for Operations for Use by the Dartmouth-Hitchcock Medical Center-Lebanon Campus and the Dartmouth College Health Service
DHMC, 2005

Developed by Kathy Kirkland, MD, Hospital
Epidemiologist, and the DHMC Readiness Committee

Background: The Readiness Plan for Epidemic Respiratory Infection (ERI) evolved from our initial response and planning for the prevention and control of Severe Acute Respiratory Syndrome (SARS) which began in the spring of 2003. During those planning activities it became clear that DHMC needs to maintain a level of readiness at all times for a variety of contagious respiratory infections with epidemic potential. Potential threats include SARS or a new strain of influenza that becomes pandemic. Many elements of the plan will make us more prepared to identify and contain other contagious respiratory infections as well, including pertussis, mycoplasma, and parainfluenza, for example.

The DHMC plan builds on guidelines from state and federal health authorities which recommend aggressive implementation of respiratory hygiene practices and universal administration of influenza vaccine to healthcare workers and high-risk patients for all healthcare facilities regardless of the presence of an epidemic.

This document outlines a plan for responding to various levels of threat posed by ERIs, and an approach to stepping up prevention and control activities as the threat increases. It is based on the premises that we should be vigilant at all times for syndromes that may represent contagious respiratory infection, and that we should maintain a group of people prepared to actively respond to changing situations by implementing appropriate parts of this plan, when indicated.

The document is divided into:

- a matrix that defines parameters that will be the critical determinants of the level of risk at DHMC
- a summary of the elements of the baseline state of readiness that should be maintained at all times
- a summary of the ways in which our surveillance, prevention and control activities may need to change at each level of increasing risk to DHMC
- an appendix that includes standard operating procedures for the management of patients who have suspected ERI as outpatients, as inpatients, and for resuscitation of these patients.

This document is intended for use by the DHMC Readiness Committee or an Incident Command team to determine actions that should be taken to prevent the spread of ERI among our patients, staff, volunteers, students, and visitors. The intent is that this document will be used in the context of advisory documents and guidance provided by NH DHHS and the CDC. It may be used as a template by other New Hampshire healthcare facilities as they prepare themselves for the threat of epidemic respiratory infection.

Epidemic Respiratory Infection ALERT MATRIX

Six levels of alert corresponding to the type of transmission, the location of the cases, and the presence and type of cases at DHMC or DC.

What type of transmission is confirmed?	Where are the cases?	Are there cases at DHMC?	Alert Level
None or sporadic cases only	Anywhere in the world	No	Ready
Person-to-person transmission	Anywhere outside the U.S. and bordering countries (Canada, Mexico)	No	Green
Person-to-person transmission	In the U.S., Canada or Mexico	No	Yellow
Person-to-person transmission	In region: NH/VT or close to borders	Does not matter	Orange
Does not matter	At DHMC or DC	Yes, but no nosocomial transmission	"Controlled Orange"
Person-to-person transmission	At DHMC or DC	Yes, with nosocomial transmission, from known sources only	Orange
Person-to-person transmission	At DHMC or DC	Yes, with nosocomial transmission, sources not clear	Red

The alert level will be determined by the Readiness Committee, using this matrix and data collected through surveillance activities. It can be upgraded (or downgraded) by the committee depending on the number of cases, or for other compelling circumstances.

At each level of alert, the Readiness Committee will consider implementing certain actions. As the level of alert becomes higher, additional actions are added to the actions initiated at the lower level.

Level: READY

Baseline activities to ensure preparedness in the absence of known active epidemic of ERI in the world

Goals

- To prevent cases of vaccine-preventable contagious respiratory infection (e.g., influenza) at DHMC and in the community.
- To promote early detection of initial cases of contagious respiratory infection (including, but not limited to influenza, SARS).
- To prevent nosocomial spread of contagious respiratory infections.
- To create systems for real-time data collection flexible enough to be adapted for use in an epidemic setting.

Influenza Vaccination

- For patients and the public
  - Nursing will carry out standing orders for all eligible patients to be offered and receive influenza vaccine in all clinics and prior to discharge from all inpatient units.
  - DHMC will continue to collaborate with other community health organizations to hold public clinics to provide influenza vaccine to all eligible community members of any age.
  - Public Affairs, with input from the Readiness Committee, will develop educational and promotional materials to promote availability and desirability of influenza vaccine for all.
  - The administering provider of flu vaccine in the inpatient and outpatient setting will document administration of influenza vaccine in CIS.
- For staff, volunteers, and students
  - Administrative, educational, and clinical leaders will promote maximum participation of staff, volunteers, and students in influenza vaccine program.
  - Occupational Medicine will provide multiple opportunities for staff, volunteers, and students to receive influenza vaccine conveniently and efficiently.
  - Occupational Medicine will present regular updates of physician compliance with flu vaccine by section for review by Board of Governors.
  - DHMC will report flu vaccine rates among direct care providers on public reporting website.

Access Control

- The Security Office will develop a plan and a timeline for implementing a policy that enables them to control access to the medical center through the use of mandatory ID badges for all staff, volunteers, students, vendors, and other people coming to DHMC to work, and a plan to lock down certain entrances and exits, and to monitor use of others, if necessary.

Surveillance, Screening and Triage

- For patients
  - Receptionists will screen all outpatients at the time of registration at selected DHMC clinics, the ED, and the Dartmouth College Health Service with the following question: Do you have a new cough that has developed over the last 10 days?, and will:
    - Provide patients who have a new cough with a surgical mask and/or tissues.
    - Document data at time of screening and transmit clinic-specific data to Infection Control each week for review and analysis of trends.
  - Clinical staff at these clinics will:
    - Evaluate patients who have a new cough or fever.
    - Place all patients who have fever and a new cough on droplet precautions, pending further evaluation.
  - The admitting office staff will screen all patients at the time of admission for "fever and cough" and will:
    - Admit patients with fever and cough to a private room with droplet precautions.
    - Document data at time of screening and transmit inpatient admitting diagnoses to Infection Control daily for review of appropriate use of precautions for inpatients.
- For staff, volunteers, and students
  - Receptionists will screen all staff, volunteers, or students who present to Occupational Medicine clinic with the following question: Do you have a new cough that has developed over the last 10 days?, and will:
    - Provide patients who have a new cough with a surgical mask and/or tissues.
    - Document data at time of screening and transmit clinic-specific data to Infection Control each week for review and analysis of trends.

- Clinical staff in Occupational Medicine clinic will:
  - Evaluate patients who have a new cough or fever.
  - Place all patients who have fever and a new cough on droplet precautions, pending further evaluation.
- Occupational Medicine staff, clinical and administrative leaders will advise staff, volunteers and students who have fever and a new cough not to come to work.
- Occupational Medicine will:
  - Screen staff, volunteers, and students who report pneumonia or respiratory infection to identify possible clusters of pneumonia or respiratory infection in healthcare providers
  - Report possible clusters to Infection Control.
- For visitors, vendors, registrants at conferences
  - Public Affairs will maintain "Ask for a Mask" signs at all entrances, and at all meeting rooms, to encourage all persons entering DHMC to self-screen (rotating the posters periodically to maintain impact).
  - Via posters, ask persons who have new cough to wear a surgical mask or use tissues to cover their mouth and nose when coughing, and to use good hand hygiene during the time they need to be at DHMC.
  - All staff will advise persons who have fever and cough to defer visiting DHMC until their illness has resolved.
- Monitoring surveillance data
  - The Infection Control Unit will monitor national, regional, and local data related to ERI and report changing trends to the Readiness Committee on a regular basis.

Infection Control/Precautions

- All staff, volunteers, and students will use *Droplet Precautions (private room and surgical mask within 3 feet of patient)* for all contact with any outpatient who has a new cough and fever, until a diagnosis of a non-contagious respiratory illness, or an infection requiring a higher level of precautions, is made.
- All staff, volunteers, and students will use *Droplet Precautions (private room and surgical mask within 3 feet of patient)* for all contact with any patient being admitted to the hospital who has a new cough and fever until a diagnosis of a non-contagious respiratory illness, or an infection requiring a higher level of precautions, is made.

- Clinic and inpatient staff will use a visible doorway "precautions sign" system to allow persons entering the room to know what type of protective equipment is needed.
- Clinic Administrative services and Housekeeping will maintain adequate supplies at all times of surgical masks, waterless hand rub, and tissues throughout public areas, clinic waiting rooms, and meeting rooms. Clinic and inpatient unit staff will maintain these supplies in clinical areas.
- The Safety Office will identify key areas throughout the hospital which need to maintain core groups of N95 respirator fit-tested personnel.
  - Each director is responsible for maintaining the appropriate number of trained and fit-tested staff
- The Safety Office will ensure that an adequate number of PAPRs are maintained for use by personnel who cannot use N95 respirators.
- Engineering will maintain negative pressure-capable rooms on 3 West.
  - Nursing will develop plans for moving patients out of these rooms on 3 West if needed.

Communication/Education

- Public Affairs will develop a sustainable and effective plan for communication and promotion of messages relating to ERI to internal and external audiences.
- Public Affairs and Communications will coordinate with the Emergency Preparedness Committee to develop an internal communication plan to allow immediate access to predefined groups of people, including "on call" staff, via e-mail, Intranet, paging system, telephone.
- The Center for Continuing Education in the Health Sciences will develop a sustainable plan to orient and educate staff regarding basic readiness activities at DHMC, and a strategy for "just-in-time" educational activities to provide timely information to providers in the event of ERI.

Additional Preparedness Activities

- The Readiness Committee will meet approximately once a month.
- The Readiness Committee will designate an Incident Command core team including senior administration, infection control, ACOS, communications, nursing, safety, engineering, security, College Health Service with 7-day a

week availability to respond to a potential outbreak of contagious respiratory infection.
- The Infection Control Unit will monitor the Health Alert Network and other communications from public health officials to review changes in recommendations from NH DHHS/CDC about screening criteria and will communicate changes to clinicians via some combination of e-mail, Intranet, or radiographic or laboratory reporting.

Level: GREEN

Confirmed efficient human-to-human transmission of potentially epidemic contagious respiratory infection present outside the U.S. and bordering countries (Canada and Mexico)

Summary: At the "GREEN" level, our basic activities remain similar to the "READY" level, except that there may be more focused surveillance and screening based on specific geographic and epidemiologic risk factors, and more aggressive forms of isolation may be required for suspected cases. Vigilance of all staff is required to identify potential cases of ERI remains critical. At the GREEN level, the following additional actions will be considered for implementation by the Readiness Committee.

Access Control

- The Readiness Committee will consider the need to activate the policy on requiring staff, volunteers, students, and vendors to wear identification while in the medical center.

Surveillance, Screening and Triage

- "Ask for a Mask" signs will be placed at all entrances, and in all meeting rooms, which may be modified to include specific risk factors for a specific ERI, to encourage all persons entering DHMC to self-screen.
  - Persons who self-identify as at risk for the designated infection are instructed to don a surgical mask and may be asked to go to a designated location for clinical evaluation.
- Receptionists in selected areas (which may expand) will continue to screen all patients at registration for new cough, and additional questions may be added if appropriate. Receptionists will:
  - Provide patients who have a new cough who have specific risk factors for the targeted infection with a surgical mask and ask clinical staff to place them immediately in a private exam room.
  - Provide patients who have a new cough but no specific risk factors for the targeted infection with a surgical mask and/or tissues.
- Clinical staff will evaluate:
  - Patients who answer "yes" to new cough and specific risk factors for fever and other symptoms, using N95 masks, gowns, gloves and eye protection.
  - Patients who answer yes to new cough but do not have specific risk factors, using droplet precautions.
- Clinicians who suspect, after initial clinical evaluation that a patient may have an ERI should immediately consult with the Infectious Disease Service and the Infection Control Unit, who will involve the state health department as appropriate. **(IF A PATIENT IS DETERMINED TO BE A SUSPECT CASE OF ERI, GO TO LEVEL: "CONTROLLED ORANGE")**
- No patient can be admitted or accepted in transfer to DHMC with a suspected diagnosis of the ERI in question, without the approval of the Infectious Disease Service.
- Staff, volunteers, and students traveling to designated high risk areas must register with Occupational Medicine upon return and report any symptoms of fever or cough that occur during a specified time period. Occupational Medicine will maintain a list of people under surveillance for this reason.

Infection Control/Precautions

- Airborne, droplet, and contact precautions are required for all contact with any outpatient who has screened as a possible ERI case, until an alternate diagnosis is made.
- Droplet precautions are required for all contact with any outpatient who has a new cough and fever, but no risk factors for the ERI, until a diagnosis of a non-contagious respiratory illness, or an infection requiring a higher level of precautions, is made.
- Any patient who has screened as a possible ERI case and requires admission to DHMC, must be admitted to a negative pressure room on 3 West, where airborne and contact precautions are required for all contact. **(IF A PATIENT IS DETERMINED TO BE A SUSPECT CASE OF ERI, GO TO LEVEL: "CONTROLLED ORANGE").**

Communication/Education

- At each committee meeting, the Readiness Committee will review the need for communication with, or educational programs for staff, volunteers, and students, and the public.

Preparedness

- The Readiness Committee meets once or twice a month, depending on the stability of the situation.

Level: YELLOW

Confirmed human-to-human transmission of potentially epidemic contagious respiratory infection documented in the U.S. or bordering countries (Canada or Mexico)

Summary: At the "YELLOW" level, the ERI is closer to home, and may pose a more real threat. Vigilance of all to identify potential cases of ERI remains critical. At the YELLOW alert level, rapid changes in the epidemiology of disease and the level of threat to DHMC may be expected. The major change is that the Readiness Committee becomes more active so that a rapid change to a higher level of alert is possible. The following additional activities will be considered.

Access Control

- Review need to require staff, volunteers, students, and vendors to wear ID badges at all times.

Surveillance, Screening and Triage

- Expand screening and triage of patients and employees to all clinics, with regular review of need to modify or add specific risk factors.
- Continued use of posters to promote screening visitors and vendors.

Infection Control/Precautions

- No changes

Communication/Education

- No changes

Preparedness

- The Readiness Committee meets at least once a week to review surveillance data and new recommendations from DHHS/CDC.

- Evaluate the availability and appropriateness of disease-specific vaccine or preventive treatment.

Level: CONTROLLED ORANGE

A case of ERI has been diagnosed at DHMC or Dartmouth College or is an inpatient at DHMC but there has been no documented nosocomial or community spread from this person to others.

Summary: When there is a patient with suspected ERI at DHMC, because of the potential for transmission in the hospital setting, the alert level immediately is raised to a form of ORANGE. (i.e., with a single imported case, we immediately would go from READY or GREEN to CONTROLLED ORANGE.) At the "CONTROLLED ORANGE" level, more caution is needed, and our activities shift from more passive to more active control measures. The goal is to prevent nosocomial spread to employees and patients within DHMC. At this level, activation of a number of new measures is considered, relating to access, screening, and clinical care, but there is an effort to maintain relatively normal operations at DHMC except in the area where a potentially infected patient is being cared for. The emphasis is on personal protection of staff and patients, and a readiness to raise the alert level quickly if there is any indication of spread.

Access Control

- Limit visitors and admissions to 3 West.
- Review need to restrict vendors, visitors, conferences.
- Require staff, volunteers, students, vendors, and other people coming to DHMC to work to wear their badges/identification at all times.

Surveillance, Screening and Triage

- Modified "Ask for a Mask" signs remain at all entrances, and at all meeting rooms, which include specific risk factors for the targeted infection, to encourage all persons entering DHMC to self-screen.
  - A knowledgeable staff member may need to be present at all entrances to assist people with self-screening, answer questions, and direct them to evaluation centers if needed.
- Screening questions for patients and employees at registration, admission will be reviewed and modified as needed at each Readiness Committee meeting.

- Staff, volunteers, and students who have had contact with suspected patients must register with Occupational Medicine and be screened daily for fever or respiratory symptoms.
- Surveillance data will be transmitted to Infection Control for review daily.

Infection Control/Precautions

- No changes

Communication/Education

- Regular updates to all staff via Intranet as determined by the Readiness Committee.

Preparedness

- Readiness Committee will meet daily to review situation and strategies.
- Nursing and ACOS will review plans for moving non-epidemic patients out of negative pressure-capable rooms on 3 West; Engineering will review plan to add HEPA filters and negative pressure to additional rooms on 3 West and ensure that the plan could be operationalized within 4 hours if needed.
- Infection Control will notify microbiology laboratory director of relevant information.

Level: ORANGE

There is evidence of nosocomial transmission of ERI from known infected patients to other patients, employees, or visitors at DHMC, OR there is human-to-human transmission in the Upper Valley region, or nearby.

Summary: "ORANGE" indicates a high level of alert, with restrictions on access to DHMC, much more active screening, and a shift away from normal operations throughout the institution. At the ORANGE level, the Readiness Committee will consider implementing each of the following additional actions.

Access Control

- All entrances to medical center will be locked except the Main Entrance, the entrance from Parking Garage, and the Emergency Department entrance.
- Security guards will be stationed at open entrances.

- Entry into facility will be restricted to the following:
  - Staff, and students with valid ID
  - Patients with appointments
  - A single adult accompanying a patient
  - A single parent of hospitalized child
- Those allowed into the facility must be screened for fever or cough (**see Surveillance, screening and triage** below) and have their temperature taken and if cleared, given something to indicate that they have been cleared to enter the facility (e.g., a sticker, a card, a stamp on their hand).
- Activities of Food Court eateries and shops, hair salon, optical shop, etc. will be suspended.
- Activities of vendors, volunteer activities, continuing education programs, except those related to the epidemic disease will be suspended.
- There will be some degree of suspension of elective surgeries, elective admissions, elective outpatient appointments as determined by the Readiness Committee.
- There will be some level of suspension of medical student rotations, construction as determined by the Readiness Committee.

Surveillance, Screening and Triage

- Patients calling for same day appointments will be screened for new cough developing over the last 10 days.
  - Patients who answer yes will be phone triaged to a clinician who can do further screening for epidemic infection risk factors and determine the need for the patient to be evaluated in person.
- Patients being called with appointment reminders will be screened for new cough and phone triaged to a clinician for further screening prior to coming to DHMC.
- All people entering DHMC will be actively screened by trained staff for cough or fever at open entrances
  - Patients and visitors who are identified to have fever and/or cough will be instructed to don a surgical mask, use waterless handrub, and go to a designated evaluation location (NB: risk factors at this alert level may be simply living in the Upper Valley, or having been at DHMC).

- Employees who have fever and/or cough will be considered possible cases:
  - If at home, they should call Occupational Medicine for evaluation prior to coming to work.
  - If at work, they should call Occupational Medicine and be instructed regarding the need for evaluation.
  - Occupational Medicine will develop a tool to screen employees regarding need for evaluation, need for home isolation, etc.
- After evaluation, no patient or employee who has fever or cough will be allowed to remain at DHMC unless the person requires hospitalization.
  - The name and phone number/address of all patients or employees sent home with suspected epidemic infection should be recorded and reported to the NH DHHS.
- Occupational Medicine will continue to maintain a log of which employees have contact with epidemic patients, whether there are unprotected exposures, and the employee's health and work status daily.

Infection Control/Precautions

- An N95 mask and contact precautions are required for all HCWs having contact with any outpatient who has fever and/or a new cough, until an alternate diagnosis is made. (This includes staff who conduct screening at DHMC entrances.)
- Adequate supplies of personal protective equipment, waterless hand rub, tissues will be maintained throughout the hospital by Housekeeping and Clinic Administrative Services, as well as clinical staff.
- Everyone providing patient care will be N95 respirator fit-tested.

Communication/Education

- Daily or more frequent updates to staff and the public/press will be provided as determined by the Readiness Committee.

Preparedness

- The Readiness Committee will meet twice daily to review infection control surveillance data, clinic operations (i.e., number of screening evaluations being done) and adequacy of new controls and revise alert level as needed.
- The Readiness Committee will reassess daily the need to create special epidemic inpatient

unit off site (e.g., Armory).
- Staff may be redeployed from areas where clinical activities have been suspended or limited to screening, infection control, Occupational Medicine, epidemic patient care and other areas of need, as determined by Readiness Committee in collaboration with hospital leaders.

Level: RED

There is evidence of untraceable or uncontrolled nosocomial transmission of ERI OR there is widespread human-to-human transmission in the Upper Valley region, or nearby

Summary: "RED" indicates the highest level of alert, with extreme restrictions on access to DHMC and a major shift away from normal operations throughout the institution. The following additional actions will be considered.

Access Control

- All entrances to medical center will be locked except one entrance designated for employees and Emergency Dept entrance.
- Security guards will be stationed at open entrances.
- Entry into facility will be restricted to the following:
  - Employee with valid ID
  - Patient arriving by ambulance [a parent may remain with a hospitalized child but cannot come and go from the medical center]
  - Patients who must receive regular, life-sustaining treatments at DHMC (e.g., dialysis patients, transfusion-dependent patients)
- Those allowed into the facility must be screened for cough and other criteria (as outlined in ORANGE) and have their temperature taken and if cleared, given something to indicate that they have been cleared to enter the facility.
- Suspension of elective surgeries, elective admissions, elective outpatient appointments, non-emergency transfers as determined by the Readiness Committee.
- Suspension of on-site student rotations, construction activities.
  - Possible redeployment of clinical students to areas of need.

Surveillance, Screening and Triage

- Required daily for all persons entering facility (see ORANGE).

Infection Control/Precautions

- All staff will wear surgical masks and use frequent hand hygiene at all times while in the facility.

Communication/Education

- There will be daily or more frequent updates to staff and the public/press as determined by the Readiness Committee.

Preparedness

- The Readiness Committee will meet twice daily to review situation.
- The Readiness Committee will reassess daily the need to create special epidemic inpatient unit off site (e.g., Armory).
- Staff may be redeployed from areas where clinical activities have been suspended or limited to screening, infection control, Occupational Medicine, epidemic patient care and other areas of need, as determined by Readiness Committee in collaboration with hospital leaders.

Appendix 1
Epidemic Respiratory Infections Patient Flow

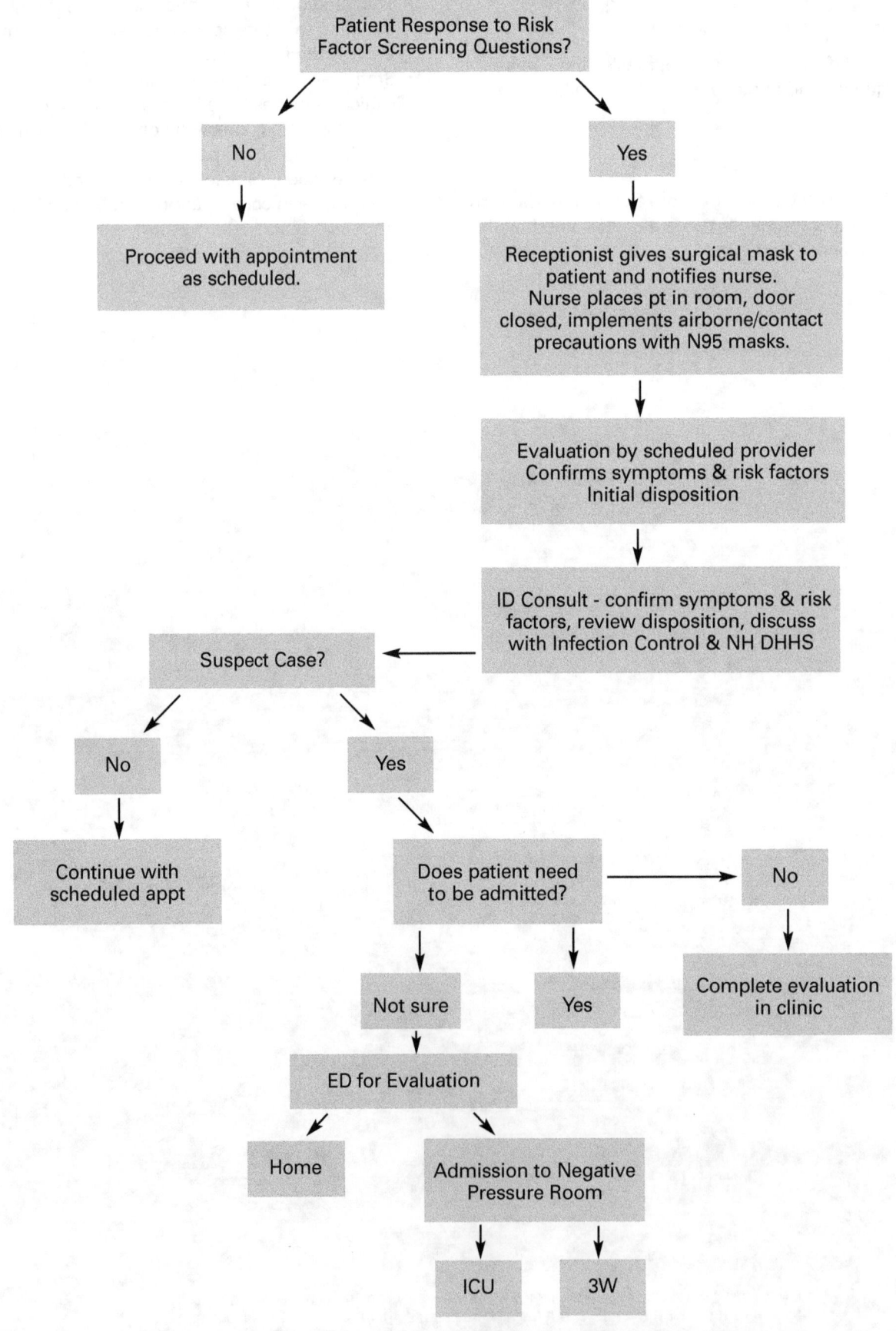

Patient Response to Risk Factor Screening Questions?

No → Proceed with appointment as scheduled.

Yes → Receptionist gives surgical mask to patient and notifies nurse. Nurse places pt in room, door closed, implements airborne/contact precautions with N95 masks.

→ Evaluation by scheduled provider Confirms symptoms & risk factors Initial disposition

→ ID Consult - confirm symptoms & risk factors, review disposition, discuss with Infection Control & NH DHHS

Suspect Case?

No → Continue with scheduled appt

Yes → Does patient need to be admitted?

No → Complete evaluation in clinic

Not sure → ED for Evaluation

Yes

ED for Evaluation → Home

→ Admission to Negative Pressure Room

→ ICU

→ 3W

Appendix 2

Suspected or Confirmed Epidemic Respiratory Infection (ERI) Outpatient Management Protocol

The following protocol will be followed when a patient has a new cough and risk factors associated with a specific epidemic respiratory infection (ERI).

Principles to follow in care of ERI patient.

- Minimize Health Care Workers (HCW) contact with the patient.
- Protect HCWs during contact with patient.
- Minimize opportunities for exposure to other patients or visitors.

Key points

1. The receptionist should give the patient a mask to put on covering their nose and mouth and immediately inform the nurse who will immediately place the patient in a private exam room, the door to the exam room must be kept closed. We want to minimize the amount of time that the patient is in the waiting area or other common areas.

2. Personnel Protective Equipment (PPE) is required for anyone going in the room to see the patient. This includes gown, gloves, goggles and N95 mask or PAPR hood. N95 masks and the PAPR hoods will be available from the Safety Office (ext. 57233) during the day or the ACOS after hours.

3. The health care provider who was scheduled to see the patient will evaluate them to confirm that they have a fever >38, respiratory symptoms and risk factors for ERI. If the provider confirms this information s/he should contact the Infectious Disease physician by calling the DHMC operator and asking for the ID physician on call.

4. The ID physician will consult with the patient's provider to confirm the suspect case and plan further evaluation. They will also notify the Infection Control Team and the NH Department of Health. If possible, a disposition decision should be made at this time.

5. If the patient is in a clinic without a negative pressure room and is considered to be a suspect case of ERI and needs further evaluation, including lab work and/or X-rays, to determine the need for hospital admission they will be moved as soon as possible to the negative air pressure room in the Emergency Department. The clinic nurse caring for the patient must call the ED (ext 57000) and notify them of this. When the patient is moved to the ED, they should be wearing a surgical mask. The patient should be taken to the ED via a route that avoids crowded public areas. The clinic nurse who has been caring for the patient will transport the patient to the ED and should continue to wear PPE.

If the patient is no longer considered to be a suspect case they may continue with their appointment as scheduled. People no longer need to follow contact and airborne isolation, only appropriate Standard Precautions.

6. The patient will remain in the negative pressure room in the ED until a decision regarding admission is made. The patient will only leave for urgent medically necessary tests that can not be done in the negative pressure room. If the patient needs to leave the ED, the charge nurse is responsible for notifying the department that they will be going to that the patient requires airborne and contact precautions. The PPE will go with the patient when they leave the ED. Employees who have contact with the patient should be kept to a minimum.

7. If the patient is stable and does not need admission the provider should coordinate appropriate medical follow-up and surveillance from the NH Department of Health prior to discharge from the clinic or ED.

8. If the patient requires admission to DHMC the Infectious Disease physician will activate the ERI plan and notify Admitting of the need to admit the patient to a negative pressure room. N95 masks and PAPR hoods will be sent with the patient. The patient will travel from the clinic or ED to the unit wearing a surgical mask via a route that avoids crowded public areas. The nurse who has been caring for the patient will transport the patient to the inpatient room and should continue to wear PPE during transport.

Appendix 3

Suspected or Confirmed Epidemic Respiratory Infections (ERI) Inpatient Management Protocol

This plan will be put into effect when a patient is believed to meet the criteria for an epidemic respiratory infection by one of the Infectious Disease physicians and needs hospitalization.

Principles to follow in care of ERI patient

- Minimize Health Care Workers (HCW) contact with the patient.
- Protect HCWs during contact with patient.
- Minimize opportunities for exposure to other patients or visitors.

Criteria for Admission

- Patient will be admitted only when medically necessary.
- Patients will not be admitted solely for the purpose of isolation.
- The Infectious Disease service must approve all admissions for ERI and is responsible for activating the ERI plan in collaboration with Infection Control.

Admitting Service/Medical Responsibility

The ERI patient will be admitted to the Hospitalist service, adult or pediatric, with mandatory consultation with Infectious Disease and Critical Care Service on admission. Transfer to the Critical Care Service should be made as soon as a patient shows signs of respiratory distress, i.e., increasing O2 requirement, FIO2 > 50, respiratory therapy assessment.

Patient Placement

All patients, adult and pediatric, will be admitted to 3W. The first case will be admitted to room 301. (If the first patient is critically ill, requiring immediate intensive care they should be admitted to a negative pressure room in the ICU for an adult or the PICU for a child.)

- Planning and activity will begin to prepare room 303 as a potential intensive care location. Engineering will install special ventilation unit to create negative pressure (Engineering Services Policy 6.207b; Temporary Negative Pressure Rooms).

Second case will be admitted to room 302.

- 3W- Pod 1 now restricted to only ERI patients. ACOS, Admitting, and nursing directors will make arrangements to move the non-ERI patients on Pod 1 to another area of the hospital.
- Engineering will install special ventilation units to create negative pressure in rooms 327, 328, and 329. Contact State of NH to get more portable HEPA filter units.
- Plan for provision of adequate staff initiated. This may require cancellation of elective cases and re-allocation of nursing staff.

ERI patients 3, 4, & 5 will be admitted to rooms 327, 328, & 329.

- When these rooms are full, 3W will be closed to all other patient types.
- Non-ERI patients will be moved to other areas of the hospital.
- Plans initiated to open an alternate site for care of ERI patients outside of MHMH.
- ERI patients will continue to be admitted to 3West until alternate care site is opened. Other units of the hospital may need to accept patients (non ERI) from 3W. Other areas of the hospital may need to close some beds in order to provide extra staff to 3W.

Any patient requiring critical care support will be placed in Room 303. Nursing staff from ICU will provide critical care in this location.

Pediatric patients will be admitted to the rooms on 3West (not the Pedi/Adolescent unit). Nursing staff from the Pedi/Adolescent unit will provide care to the pediatric patient on 3West.

If the number of ERI patients exceeds the number of available private negative pressure rooms patients with known ERI can be cohorted together. The following patients will be given priority for the private negative pressure rooms; these decisions will be made in collaboration with the ACOS, Infectious Disease, Infection Control, and Admitting.

- ERI patients who are known to have transmitted ERI to others.
- Patients who are being assessed for ERI (do not want to put someone who does not ultimately have ERI in with known ERI patients).

As soon as the Admissions Department is aware of ERI patient admission they will notify the ACOS (ext 5-8245 or beeper # 9732) of the admission.

The ACOS will work with Admitting and the 3W staff to expedite the admission. (The patient will remain where s/he has been evaluated until the inpatient room is ready.) The ACOS will:

- Expedite transferring current patient to another room
- Notify engineering of the admission, engineering will ensure negative pressure is functioning in the room (This can be done by holding a small strip of tissue paper at the closed door and observing to be sure that it is pulled toward the room, not blown out away from the room. Engineering can assist with this if needed.)
- Ensure the room's pressure monitor alarm has been turned on and is working. Use the key to turn the room pressure monitor to "Infectious Isolation - Negative Pressure". This only turns the room alarm on, the room is always on negative pressure and does not need to be turned on. The alarm should go on when the door is left open for more than 1 minute or the seal is not adequate to maintain negative pressure in the room. Before the patient arrives to the room, check the room pressure monitor to be sure it is working by opening door, the alarm should go off after 1 minute. If there are questions about the monitor or room call Engineering. Monday through Friday 0800-1600 Ext. 5-7150. At other times use Engineering Pager #9234.
- Ensure unnecessary equipment (extra chairs, cot) is removed from the room
- Ensure that protective equipment is available in the anteroom (masks, gowns, goggles, gloves, PAPR units); Masks and goggles can be obtained from Stores, gowns from Linen Service ext. 57136, and PAPR units are in the Emergency Department. If rooms without an anteroom are used for a ERI patient the necessary equipment will need to be set up on a cart outside the room.

Patient Transport
Guidelines for moving ERI patients in DHMC
- The nurse caring for the patient will transport the patient with the assistance of transportation personnel as needed.
- If an elevator is needed, use a service elevator and be sure there are no other people in it.
- The patient must wear a surgical mask over their nose and mouth during transport through the institution.

- Security (ext. 5-7896) can help with providing an empty elevator available and other logistics if needed.
- Employees who are transporting the patient should wear gloves, N95 mask (or PAPR hood and motor unit), goggles, and gown.

Protective Equipment
Anyone entering the room must wear respiratory protection appropriate to the disease. If the disease is transmitted via the airborne route then the following is required.

- N95 mask (employee must have been fitted and trained by an administrator of the Respiratory Protection Program) and goggles (face shields are not felt to provide adequate protection).
- If the employee cannot be fitted for an N95 mask they must wear a PAPR unit when entering the room. (People wearing a PAPR hood do not need goggles; the hood provides protection for the eyes.)
- Everyone must wear gloves and a gown.

When leaving the room the PPE will be removed in the anteroom, if there is one, or just outside the door if the room does not have an anteroom. Remove PPE in the following order.

- Untie the gown's waist tie
- Remove gloves and dispose of them in trash
- Remove goggles handling them by the side pieces and place in sink
- Remove mask handling it by the head straps and dispose of in trash
- Untie neck ties of gown and carefully remove gown turning sleeves inside out as arms are pulled out, place gown in linen bag
- Put new gloves on and disinfect goggles with alcohol or Dimension III
- Remove gloves and dispose
- WASH HANDS before doing anything else.

People who have used a PAPR unit should remove PPE in the following order:

- Remove hood and motor unit and place on chux pad
- Remove gloves, dispose of them in trash and put new gloves on, clean hood, hose and motor with Dimension III, place unit in clean area and dispose of chux pad
- Untie the gown's waist tie
- Remove gloves and dispose of them in trash
- Untie neck ties of gown and carefully remove gown turning sleeves inside out as arms are

pulled out, place gown in linen bag.
• WASH HANDS before doing anything else.

All of the PPE, except for the PAPR units, are either disposable or single use and should not be reused.

N95 masks will not be reused. They will be disposed in the trash of as soon as they are removed.

PAPR units must be disinfected as soon as they are removed. The person who used the equipment is responsible for cleaning it and plugging in the motor unit to recharge while it is not in use. The hood and hose must be wiped with a disinfectant before being handled and used again. The motor unit should be wiped with a disinfectant if it has been in contact with respiratory secretions.

Room Setup
Both doors to rooms 301 and 302 must be kept closed. When other rooms are used, the single door to the room must be kept closed.

Only essential equipment should be in the room. Equipment brought into the room should be left in the room for use only by that patient. Thermometer, stethoscope glucometer, pulse oyx, should remain in the room. A thermometer can be obtained from CSR, a glucometer can be obtained from Point of Care Testing, ext 57198, in the lab, pulse oyx can be obtained from respiratory therapy. Equipment that cannot be left in the room must be disinfected before it is used for any other patient. Most equipment can be disinfected by cleaning thoroughly with Dimension III.

Linen requires no special precautions. Used linen should be handled as little as possible. It should be carefully rolled together in a manner that avoids shaking, and placed in the yellow linen bags.

Trash requires no special precautions. Routine waste should be placed in the regular trash bags. Any waste that is saturated with blood or body fluids should be disposed of in the tan bags.

Regular dishes will be used. The dietary aide will give the tray to the nurse who will bring it into the room. The nurse will also bring the tray out of the room when the meal is finished.

Blood and other specimens may be sent to the lab via normal mechanisms. Be sure the outside of the biohazard bag does not become contaminated.

The patient room should be cleaned daily and as needed by housekeeping. While the patient is in the room the housekeeping staff must wear N95 mask and goggles or a PAPR unit and gloves and gowns while in the room. Routine cleaning with a disinfectant is adequate. When the patient is discharged the room should be left closed for an hour, then people may enter without masks to clean.

Staffing
Nursing staff from Pediatrics and the Critical Care units will provide care to pediatric or critical care patients on 3W.

The registered nurse taking care of a ERI patient will not care for any other patients. Other staff members such as LNAs who may be needed to assist with care may care for other patients.

The goal is to limit the number of employees who enter the room while providing appropriate safe care for the patient.

All employees will be expected to participate in the care of ERI patients as needed.

Pregnant employees will not be excused from caring for ERI patients.

Staff who are taking care of ERI patients may wear hospital supplied scrub uniforms. (There is a cabinet in Stores that has a few scrubs available for emergency use, a larger supply will need to be ordered from the linen department.)

Staff who have cared for a ERI patient may shower in their locker room before leaving work.

Employee Surveillance
A list of all employees who enter the room or have had close contact with the patient will be started by Infection Control as soon as the ERI plan is activated and maintained by the RN who is assigned to the patient. All employees entering the room or who have contact with the ERI patient must add their name and contact information to the list. The unit secretary will FAX the prior day's list to Occupational Medicine (FAX 650-0928) between 8:00 and 9:00 a.m. each day. These employees will be followed by Occupational Medicine for symptoms of the disease. Occupation Medicine will develop a disease-specific protocol for close monitoring of all employees who have had contact with the ERI patient.

Visitors
No visitors. People can talk to the patient via telephone.

For pediatric patients, one parent may be allowed in the room. They will need to use PPE and follow policies as above. They may not sleep in the room.

Special Situations
Cough inducing or aerosol producing procedures (intubation, sputum induction, nebulizer treatment, CPAP, BiPAP, suctioning) should not be done unless

absolutely necessary. If they must be done the patient should be medicated if possible to limit aerosol production (sedate, paralyze). The absolute minimum number of employees should be in the room. Employees who are in the room during such a procedure must wear PAPR units.

To the extent possible all tests and procedures will be done in the patient's room. Medically necessary tests that cannot be done in the patient's room need to be planned and coordinated with the department doing the test so that the patient does not wait in the department's waiting area, as few staff as possible are present and they have appropriate PPE, as few other patients as possible are in the area. The room and equipment must be appropriately cleaned after the patient leaves and before another patient is seen.

If surgery is needed it should be done at a time when as few other patients as possible are in the OR. The patient should be brought directly into the OR, not wait in the holding area. As few staff as possible should be in the room. The OR staff in the room should all wear N95 masks and goggles as well as other appropriate PPE.

If the patient needs dialysis, this will be done in the patient's room. The patient will not go to the dialysis unit.

In the event of cardiopulmonary arrest a Protected Code Blue will be called. Only 6 members of the code team will be in the room. They must all wear the appropriate PPE; PAPR unit, gloves and gown. Equipment and supplies must go in only one direction (equipment and supplies that are taken off the code cart are not put back on the cart).

Cohorting of Patients and Staff

If there is significant ERI transmission in the facility or frequent unprotected exposures then patients and staff may need to be cohorted in separate areas of the facility according to their exposure status;

- No exposure
- Unprotected exposure but no symptoms
- Unprotected exposure with symptoms but do not meet the ERI case definition
- Symptoms meet the ERI case definition

This policy has been reviewed and accepted by

Hospitalist Service _____

Critical Care Service _____

Pediatric Service _____

Infectious Disease Service _____

Occupational Medicine Department _____

Emergency Department _____

GIM Clinic _____

Admitting Department _____

ACOS _____

Nursing Director for 3W _____

Nursing Director for Pediatrics _____

Nursing Director for Critical Care _____

Housekeeping Department _____

Engineering _____

Perioperative Services _____

CPR Committee _____

Respiratory Therapy _____

Security _____

Transportation _____

Laboratory _____

Risk Management _____

Appendix D
Self-Triage and Home Care Resources for Healthcare Workers and Patients

Appendix D-1
Sample Self-Triage Algorithm for Persons with Influenza Symptoms

Reproduced with permission from the Department of Veterans Affairs, VA Pandemic Influenza Plan Appendix E-5: SAMPLE Self-Triage Algorithm for Persons with Influenza Symptoms.

You may have influenza (flu).
When should you seek additional help from a healthcare provider?

The symptoms of influenza are:

- Fever—low (99°F) to high (104°F), usually for 3 days, but may persist for 4 to 8 days. Sometimes fever will go away and return a day later.
- Aching muscles
- Cough
- Headache
- Joint aches
- Eye pain
- Feeling very cold or having shaking chills
- Feeling very tired
- Sore throat, runny or stuffy nose

If you have some of these symptoms:

Stay Home
- Rest
- Drink Fluids
- Take fever reducers (acetaminophen or ibuprofen)

But IF you

- Are unable to drink enough fluids (urine becomes dark; you may feel dizzy when standing)
- Have fever for more than 3 to 5 days
- Feel better, than develop a fever again

Or IF you

- Become short of breath or you develop wheezing
- Cough up blood
- Have pain in your chest with breathing
- Have heart disease (like angina, or congestive heart failure) and you develop chest pain
- Become unable to walk or sit up, or function normally (others might be the ones to notice this-especially in elderly persons)

CALL your healthcare provider

GO RIGHT AWAY for healthcare

Appendix D-2
Home Care Guide for Influenza

Reproduced with permission from the Department of Veterans Affairs, VA Pandemic Influenza Plan Appendix E-6, Home Care Guide for Influenza: Symptom and Care Log, Infection Control Measures for the Home.

A person with influenza will often become ill very suddenly. Fever and the worst symptoms often last three days, but sometimes last as many as eight days. The person may feel weak, tired, or less energetic than normal for weeks afterward, and may have a long-lasting hacking cough.

Common symptoms:
Fever—low (99°F) to high (104°F), usually for 3 days, but may persist for 4 to 8 days. Sometimes fever will go away and return a day later.
- Extreme fatigue
- Muscle and body aches
- Feeling very cold or having shaking chills
- Joint aches
- Headache (may be severe)
- Eye pain
- Sore throat
- Stuffed nose or runny nose
- Dry cough initially, may become a deep, hacking, and painful cough over the course of several days
- No appetite for food or desire to drink fluids

Supplies to have on hand:
- Thermometer
- Acetaminophen
- Cough suppressants/cough syrup
- Drinks—fruit juices, sports drinks
- Light foods—clear soups, crackers, applesauce
- Blankets; warm covers

Caring for a person with influenza:
- Comfort measures
  - Have the patient rest in bed.
  - Allow the sick person to judge the amount of bed covers needed; when fever is high the person may feel very cold and want several blankets.
  - Give acetaminophen or ibuprofen according to the package label or a health care provider's direction to reduce fever, headache, and muscle, joint or eye pain.
- Fluids—give frequently, extremely important to replace body fluids that are lost as a result of fever.
- Feeding
  - Give light foods as the person wants: fluids are more important than food, especially in the first days when the fever may be highest.

When to seek additional medical advice:
- If the person is short of breath or breathing rapidly at rest
- If the person's skin is dusky or bluish in color
- If the person is disoriented ("out of it")
- If the person is so dizzy or weak that standing is difficult (in a person who was able to walk before the illness)
- If the person has not urinated in 12 or more hours

Symptom and Care Log for Home Care
(Copy, fill out, and bring log sheets to healthcare provider visits)

Name of patient _____

Name of healthcare provider _____

Date	Time	Observations*	Temperature	Medication

* How the person looks; what the person is doing; fluids or foods taken since the last observation.

Appendix E
References for Diagnosis and Treatment of Staff During an Influenza Pandemic

Please refer to www.pandemicflu.gov or http://www.pandemicflu.gov/vaccine/#testing for current information and recommendations. Reproduced from the CDC Influenza (Flu) Laboratory Diagnostic Procedures for Influenza webpage, http://www.cdc.gov/flu/professionals/labdiagnosis.htm. Last accessed March 6, 2007.

Appendix E-1. Influenza Diagnostic Table

Procedure	Influenza Types Detected	Acceptable Specimens	Time for Results	Rapid result available
Viral culture	A and B	NP swab[2], throat swab, nasal wash, bronchial wash, nasal aspirate, sputum	3-10 days [3]	No
Immunofluorescence DFA Antibody Staining	A and B	NP swab[2], nasal wash, bronchial wash, nasal aspirate, sputum	2-4 hours	No
RT-PCR5	A and B	NP swab[2], throat swab, nasal wash, bronchial wash, nasal aspirate, sputum	2-4 hours	No
Serology	A and B	paired acute and convalescent serum samples[6]	>2 weeks	No
Enzyme Immuno Assay (EIA)	A and B	NP swab[2], throat swab, nasal wash, bronchial wash	2 hours	No
Rapid Diagnostic Tests				
Directigen Flu A[7] (Becton-Dickinson)	A	NP wash and aspirate	<30 minutes	Yes
Directigen Flu A+B[7,9] (Becton-Dickinson)	A and B	NP swab[2],aspirate, wash; lower nasal swab; throat swab; bronchioalveolar lavage	<30 minutes	Yes
Directigen EZ Flu A+B[7,9] (Becton-Dickinson)	A and B	NP swab[2], aspirate, wash; lower nasal swab; throat swab; bronchioalveolar lavage	<30 minutes	Yes
FLU OIA4,7 (Biostar)	A and B	NP swab[2], throat swab, nasal aspirate, sputum	<30 minutes	Yes
FLU OIA A/B [7, 9] (Biostar)	A and B	NP swab[2], throat swab, nasal aspirate, sputum	<30 minutes	Yes
XPECT Flu A&B[7,9] (Remel)	A and B	Nasal wash, NP swab[2], throat swab	<30 minutes	Yes
NOW Influenza A[8,9] (Binax)	A	Nasal wash/aspirate, NP swab[2]	<30 minutes	Yes
NOW Influenza B[8,9] (Binax)	B	Nasal wash/aspirate, NP swab[2]	<30 minutes	Yes
NOW Influenza A&B[8,9] (Binax)	A and B	Nasal wash/aspirate, NP swab[2]	<30 minutes	Yes
OSOM® Influenza A&B[9] (Genzyme)	A and B	Nasal swab	<30 minutes	Yes
QuickVue Influenza Test[4,8] (Quidel)	A and B	NP swab[2], nasal wash, nasal aspirate	<30 minutes	Yes

QuickVue Influenza A+B Test[8,9] (Quidel)	A and B	NP swab[2], nasal wash, nasal aspirate	<30 minutes	Yes
SAS Influenza A Test[7,8,9]	A	NP wash2, NP aspirate[2]	<30 minutes	Yes
SAS Influenza B Test[7,8,9]	B	NP wash2, NP aspirate[2]	<30 minutes	Yes
ZstatFlu[4,8] (ZymeTx)	A and B	throat swab	<30 minutes	Yes

1. List may not include all test kits approved by the U.S. Food and Drug Administration.

2. NP = nasopharyngeal.

3. Shell vial culture, if available, may reduce time for results to 2 days.

4. Does not distinguish between influenza A and B virus infections.

5. RT-PCR = reverse transcriptase polymerase chain reaction.

6. A fourfold or greater rise in antibody titer from the acute- (collected within the 1st week of illness) to the convalescent-phase (collected 2-4 weeks after the acute sample) sample is indicative of recent infection.

7. Moderately complex test – requires specific laboratory certification.

8. CLIA-waived test. Can be used in any office setting. Requires a certificate of waiver or higher laboratory. certification.

9. Distinguishes between influenza A and B virus infections.

Disclaimer: Use of trade names or commercial sources is for identification only and does not imply endorsement by the Centers for Disease Control and Prevention or the Department of Health and Human Services.

Appendix F
Pandemic Planning Checklists and Example Plans

1. Hospital Preparedness Checklist (Department of Health and Human Services)
   http://www.hhs.gov/pandemicflu/plan/sup3.html#app2

2. Long-term Care and Other Residential Facilities Pandemic Influenza Planning Checklist
   (Department of Health and Human Services)
   http://www.pandemicflu.gov/plan/LongTermCareChecklist.html

3. Medical Offices and Clinics Pandemic Influenza Planning Checklist
   (Department of Health and Human Services)
   http://www.pandemicflu.gov/plan/medical.html

4. Emergency Medical Services and Non-emergent (Medical) Transportation Organizations
   Pandemic Influenza Planning Checklist
   (Department of Health and Human Services)
   http://www.pandemicflu.gov/plan/emgncy medical.html

5. Home Health Care Services Pandemic Influenza Planning Checklist
   (Department of Health and Human Services)
   http://www.pandemicflu.gov/plan/healthcare.html

6. Department of Veterans Affairs (VA)
   VA Pandemic Influenza Plan Appendix D-2: Sample Emergency Management Program
   Standard Operating Procedure (SOP)
   http://www.publichealth.va.gov/flu/pandemicflu_plan.htm#

Appendix F-1
Sample Emergency Management Program Standard Operating Procedure (SOP)
Reproduced with permission from the Department of Veterans Affairs Pandemic Plan, Appendix D-2: Sample Emergency Management Program Standard Operating Procedure (SOP).

Pandemic Influenza Affecting A VA Healthcare Facility *(Modify for your facility)*

Emergency Management Program Guidebook Department of Veterans Affairs

THE DEPARTMENT OF VETERANS AFFAIRS MEDICAL CENTER (LOCATION)

EMERGENCY MANAGEMENT PROGRAM (DATE) STANDARD OPERATING PROCEDURE NO. ( )

SUBJECT: VA Health Care Facility's Preparation and Response to an Influenza Pandemic

Description of the Threat/Event.
    a. *Agent.* A pandemic occurs when a new strain of influenza virus emerges that has the ability to infect and be passed between humans. Because humans would have little immunity to the new virus, a worldwide epidemic, or pandemic, can ensue. Influenza viruses have threatened the health of human populations for centuries. The diversity and propensity of influenza viruses for mutation have thwarted efforts to develop both a universal vaccine and highly effective antiviral drugs. As a result, and despite annual vaccination programs and modern medical technology, even seasonal influenza in the United States results in approximately 36,000 deaths and 226,000 hospitalizations each year. A pandemic strain of influenza could cause manyfold more. Transmission of influenza is aided by the fact that infected people may shed virus and spread the infection for one-half day to one day *before* symptoms begin.
    b. *Clinical Disease.* Symptoms of influenza typically begin two days after exposure, often starting with a sudden onset of fever, severe fatigue or muscle pain, sore throat, and a dry cough. Uncomplicated seasonal influenza commonly leads to three to five days of acute illness, including fever and prostration, leaving the sufferer feeling weakened and with a residual cough for two or more weeks longer. A

new strain may present a different clinical course and be much more serious, causing severe morbidity and mortality from influenza pneumonia or pneumonitis and secondary bacterial infections.
    c. *Public Health Response.* Public health measures to slow or stop a pandemic influenza will likely include a number of actions that will have a range of success. A monovalent influenza vaccine made for the specific pandemic strain will be manufactured, but this will take several months. An antiviral medication, oseltamivir, that can be given to exposed persons to prevent illness and help limit transmission is available but supplies are limited and manufacturing is a complex process. Oseltamivir may be effective against the H5N1 avian influenza that has infected humans in Asia and Europe; VA holds a 500,000 treatment course stockpile of oseltamivir. Other public health measures include commonsense actions, like hand washing, respiratory hygiene, staying home when sick, and using telework or telecommuting options when able. Health care facility actions involve isolating the sick, having staff wear appropriate personal protective equipment (PPE), and screening for influenza illness or exposure before permitting entry to a facility. Community, regional, and nationally-mandated measures may include declaration of "snow days", postponing of large public gatherings, quarantine of the exposed, and restrictions on travel.

Impact on Mission Critical Systems.
* An influenza pandemic can quickly overwhelm a VA medical center's or community-based outpatient clinic's normal capacity to provide timely and accessible medical care. Because of the ease with which influenza is transmitted, healthcare facilities can quickly become sites of intensive exposure for staff and non-infected patients. Breaks in procedure or unanticipated exposures may overwhelm a whole Medical Center, for example, by exposing personnel and requiring quarantine of the Medical Center. For this reason it is incumbent that VHA facilities prepare for the possibility of an influenza pandemic.
* An influenza pandemic can quickly overwhelm a hospital's or CBOC's mission critical systems, causing such problems as:
* Staffing shortages from community quarantine and competing family interests.

- Depleted supplies of vaccines and antivirals.
- Stretched bed capacity and operational space required for patient care or quarantine.
- A pandemic, by definition, will be a wide-spread—even national—event, so close coordination and cooperation with local, county, state public health agencies; and private sector healthcare facilities will be necessary and vital. It will also be necessary for VA medical centers to anticipate VA's mission to back up the Department of Defense (and provide care to designated members of the military) and VA's responsibilities to the National Response Plan (and provide care and resources for care to non-enrolled veterans and non-veterans).

Operating Units and Key Personnel with Responsibility to Manage this Threat.

- *Facility Director* – Responsible for assuring the organization implements the necessary preparatory measures for a potential influenza pandemic. The Director is also responsible for initiating the organization's disaster plan.
- *Infection Control Team/Epidemiology* – Key role in: tracking potential and confirmed cases; infection control management of patients using airborne precautions (private room, negative airflow, N95 respirator use by staff) or, when the Medical Center is overwhelmed, using droplet precautions and cohorting (isolation of infectious patients together, but away from non-exposed); working with and reporting to local and state public health agencies; serving as a VA medical center information resource on changing public health recommendations and on the community/outbreak; assisting with vaccination decisions affecting staff and patients; and advising on mass distribution systems for vaccine and antivirals.
- *Engineering Service* – Key role in: assessment of negative airflow rooms and negative airflow systems; identification of areas suitable for cohorting patients both in waiting areas and after hospitalization.
- *Clinical Laboratory* – Key role in: obtaining and performing diagnostic tests for the pandemic strain; knowing availability of reference laboratories for diagnosis (like the CDC's Laboratory Response Network [LRN] or state laboratories); advising on specimen collection; safe handling, storage, and shipping of specimens.
- *Safety/Industrial Hygiene* – Key role in: support of N95 respirator usage (fit testing) program.

- *Police and Security* – Key role in: crowd control, managing the flow of patients and visitors. If the situation warrants, police have key role in perimeter control, site access. Police may be called upon to protect the supply of influenza vaccines and supplies like oseltamivir, vaccine, N95 masks, and surgical or procedure-type masks. Perimeter access and site control may pertain to staff, staff relatives/family, and patients and require ingress and egress control. Site control may include assisting with drive-through triage stations or drive-through clinic sites, and mass distribution of vaccine and antivirals.
- *Medical Service* – Key role in: clinical diagnosis of cases; treatment of cases; providing healthcare advice via telephone; staffing innovative care delivery sites, advising/assisting with mass delivery of vaccine and antivirals.
- *Nursing Service* – Key roles in: staffing and bed support for inpatient, outpatient, and innovative care delivery sites; assisting with restriction of non-essential personnel from patient rooms (i.e., environmental management service, nutrition and food service personnel); providing healthcare advice via telephone; advising/assisting with mass delivery of vaccine and antivirals.
- *Emergency Department* – Key role in: monitoring incoming patients suspected of exposure or disease; making decisions on maintaining separate clinical activities.
- *Pharmacy* – Key role in managing the supply of vaccines and antivirals.
- *Employee/Occupational Health* – Key role in: employee vaccination/clinical care (identification of vaccine contraindications), information flow/risk communication to staff; advising/assisting with advice to staff about their ability to work, maintaining healthcare records for staff, including immune status.
- *EMS/Safety* – Key role in: advising on cleaning of rooms; equipment; communication of advice on cleaning measures.
- *Volunteer Service* – Key role in: coordinating volunteers (existing and community members) willing to assist. Volunteers also should assist in establishing an area for child care and respite for healthcare facility staff unable to leave the facility.
- *Public Affairs* – Key role in: keeping staff and patients informed, updating website, working with VSOs, media.

Mitigation/Preparedness Activities of the Threat/Event.

The mode(s) of transmission, degree of morbidity and mortality, and amount of societal disruption that a pandemic influenza might cause will be uncertain until the specific influenza strain is identified and observed. From applying what is known about seasonal influenza, it might be expected that a pandemic influenza would follow some of the same transmission patterns: ready transmission by respiratory droplets (and perhaps by aerosolized particles) from person to person; shedding and transmission of virus before persons are ill, a short incubation period of approximately 2 days, and thus a potential doubling of cases every 2 to 3 days.

a. *Hazard Reduction.*
- Notification/risk communications plan.
- Activation of hospital emergency plan.
- Perimeter control potential: need for increased security staffing, heightened security requirements for access control.
- Building systems assessment for cohorting potential and confirmed patients.
- Implementation of measures to provide added capacity for a potential surge of inpatient and ambulatory care.
- Exposure control/Infection control: Airborne Infection Isolation and Contact Precautions are advised for a potentially lethal strain of pandemic influenza, in order to maximally protect staff. Patients should be placed in room with negative airflow and HEPA exhaust; and should wear surgical masks when transported through the Medical Center. If facilities are unable to exercise this degree of isolation, cohorting of patients in common, exposed areas with HVAC isolation and exhaust (if possible) and use of respiratory droplet precautions by staff are advised.
- Separation of new, unexposed patients from potential pandemic influenza cases.
- Use of Airborne Infection Isolation and Contact Precautions, if possible, or Droplet Precautions.
- Visitor restriction policies.
- If necessary, control of the perimeter: need for increased security staffing, heightened security requirements for access control.

b. *Preparedness Strategies and Resources.*
- Establishment of Pandemic Response Team that will be prepared to work during a pandemic.
- Vaccination (if available).
- Antiviral medications prescribed to prevent illness in the exposed or unvaccinated (if available).
- Public health measures of hand washing, respiratory hygiene, staying home when ill, respecting quarantine, isolation, "snow day" and travel, and public gathering limitations.
- Education (on public health measures, infection control guidelines, home care, self-triage [to determine when medical care is necessary]).
- Plan for Airborne Infection Isolation and Contact Precautions for all personnel with patient contact.
- Anticipation of need to manage a large number of fatalities.

Response/Recovery from the Event/Threat.
a. *Hazard Control and Monitoring Strategies.*
- First case identified at a VAMC.
  1. Should be immediately reported: any suspected case(s) of pandemic influenza to Infection Control for confirmation. Infection Control would then brief the Chief of Medicine and the Chief of Staff. If case is confirmed, the Director, Safety Officer, Police and Occupational Health would be notified (this will most likely occur when a known pandemic virus is circulating elsewhere in the world and a VA medical center suspects it has the first U.S. or regional case).
  2. Activate Infection Control Team for initiation of patient/exposed staff tracking system, patient/staff educational information.
  3. Clear all patients and employees from the vicinity of the suspected case.
  4. Document details of incident and names of all persons within the immediate "at risk" area (i.e., who have become contacts and may require quarantine, antiviral medications).
  5. Contact local/state public health contacts for diagnostic sample collection and shipping instructions.

6. Contact local/state public health agencies, Pharmacy Benefits Management, or VACO Office of Public Health and Environmental Hazards to obtain vaccine, depending on guidance provided at the time (if pandemic vaccine is available).
7. Contact Pharmacy Benefits Management, or VACO Office of Public Health and Environmental Hazards for access to VA's oseltamivir (antiviral medication) stockpile.
8. Activate Infection Control Team for initiation of patient/exposed employee tracking system, patient/employee educational information.
9. Initiate antiviral medication for all potential exposed persons as appropriate after discussion with local/state public health agencies, if appropriate.
10. Notify internal personnel, as appropriate, including Chief of Staff, Health Care Providers, Nursing Service, Pharmacy, Microbiology Laboratory, and Engineering for immediate inventory of critical resources.
11. Immediately assess potential impact of actual event on mission-critical systems to include staffing, critical supplies, operational space, potential for patient and staff exposures and HVAC system.

◦ Cases already identified among existing enrolled veterans.
1. VA personnel must maintain communications and awareness with local and state public health agencies of progression of the pandemic in the community. Information must be shared with internal VA personnel, including VAMC Director, Chief of Staff, Police and Security, Chief Nurse Executive, Safety Officer/Industrial Hygienist, Employee/Occupational Health, Emergency Room Personnel, Health Care Providers, Pharmacy, and Microbiology Laboratory for immediate inventory of critical resources.
    A. Perform active surveillance for pandemic influenza appearing among hospitalized inpatients, or outpatients according to the prevailing case definition.
    B. Notify the Clinical Microbiology Laboratory of potential for use of rapid diagnostic tests or sending of specimens to reference laboratories.

C. Immediately assess potential impact of reported community events on mission critical systems to include staffing, critical supplies and operational space.
D. Await follow-up information from local authorities and prepare for potential presentation of patients.

b. *Resource Issues.*
◦ Staffing needs will be monitored and addressed by Chief of Staff, Chief of Nursing, VAMC Director, and other involved Service Chiefs.
◦ Critical Supplies – Vaccine (if available at the time) will likely be distributed through state health departments or through VA Central Office Pharmacy Benefits Management Strategic Healthcare Group. Additional timely information about vaccine may be expected from VACO. Other critical supplies to assess in the event of pandemic influenza include respiratory support equipment (oxygen, and oxygen-delivery equipment, ventilators), personal protective equipment, antimicrobial soap and alcohol-based hand cleaners, antibiotics to treat secondary bacterial pneumonias, morgue kits.
◦ Resource Allocation – Develop criteria and transparent processes for allocation decisions regarding resources that may not be available in sufficient quantities during a pandemic: antivirals, respirators, vaccines, staff.
◦ Space Management – Assess negative airflow room and cohorting bed and space availability; refrigerated space to store bodies.
◦ Emergency Room capabilities, acute care clinic capabilities and current/projected bed availability should be immediately assessed.
◦ Exposed patients and staff might expect short-term quarantine on site or relocation to alternate care sites or alternate healthcare facilities.
◦ Consideration should be given to providing pandemic influenza countermeasures that are in short supply to staff members' families (vaccine, antivirals, personal protective equipment), depending on availability and on the facility's responsibilities and assignments under the National Response Plan. If staff members' families can be protected, staff will be more available to take care of patients.

c. *Clinical Response.*
- Treatment protocols will be based upon prevailing knowledge of the pandemic influenza strain and will include supportive care (respiratory support, hemodynamic support) and use of antivirals.
- Clinical admission/treatment decisions will be made by the health care providers.
- All quarantine and visitor restriction decisions will be made by the VAMC Director based upon recommendations of the Infection Control Team or pandemic influenza response team following local/state public health guidance and decisions, and advice of regional VA counsel, if needed. Such decisions will be proportional to the disease impact, necessary, relevant, and applied equitably, and will employ the least restrictive means if options are available.
- All patients treated and evaluated for potential pandemic influenza must be reported to the Infection Control Team or designated pandemic influenza response team for data collection.
- Patient and staff recordkeeping must be maintained according to usual standards, if possible.
- The Infection Control Team or designated pandemic influenza response team will monitor all potential cases and make appropriate reports to the VAMC Director and state and local public health agencies.

Notes:
1. Vaccination of Health Care Providers: Vaccine for a pandemic influenza strain will be developed once the strain is known. This vaccine will most likely be distributed to states and then to public and private medical centers. Changes and updates on vaccine availability will be communicated to VISNs and VAMCs from VACO.
    i. The Infection Control Team, or designated pandemic influenza response team, working with the Chief of Staff and VAMC Director will notify Health Care Providers when treatment/exposure guidelines are updated or as new resources are made available. The Infection Control Team can monitor the VA pandemic influenza websites

for these updates. Note that VA guidance may differ from CDC guidance.

d. *Recovery Strategies.*
- Periodic critical supply inventories with re-supply or supplementation from outside facilities, as needed.
- Periodic staffing census with workload redistribution, as needed.
- Close monitoring of patient census and bed status.
- Monitoring of staff and patient mental health.

External Notification Procedures.
a. *Within VA.* VISN, VACO.
b. *Other State and Federal Agencies.* Local and state public health departments who will notify CDC.
- OSHA – follow prevailing rules for notification of employee fatalities and hospitalizations.
c. Community Entities. Neighboring hospitals, emergency response systems (police, firefighters, emergency medical services, 911 operators).

Specialized Staff Training.
- Health Care Provider Training – Recognition of clinical syndromes associated with influenza, treatment protocols, guidelines for personal protective equipment.
- Infection Control Team Training – Passive and active surveillance systems for monitoring reportable infectious disease pathogens.
- Safety Specialist/Industrial Hygienist – N95 respirator usage.
- Clinical Laboratories – Diagnostic tests, specimen collection, handling, and shipping.
- Social Work Service – Introductory training on pandemic influenza, risks, treatments, family implications, and follow-up.
- Police and Security – Introductory training on pandemic influenza, PPE recommendations.
- Environmental Management Service Personnel – Introductory training on pandemic influenza risks, decontamination of environments, bedclothing management, PPE recommendations.

References and Further Assistance.
- The VA Pandemic Influenza Plan.
- The VA Respiratory Infectious Diseases Emergency Plan (an amendment to the VHA Emergency Management Guidebook).

Available at http://www.publichealth.va.go/
watch/respiratoryID.htm
- VHA Under Secretary for Health Influenza
Advisories. Available at http://www.
publichealth.va.gov/flu/advisory.htm
- Local, County, State Health Departments (24/7
contact information must be part of your emergency plans for pandemic influenza).
- VA guidance and websites on pandemic
influenza www.publichealth.va.gov/infection
dontpassiton
http://www.publichealth.va.gov/flu/
pandemicflu.htm

- Federal websites on pandemic influenza
www.pandemicflu.gov
- Phone Numbers.
  - VACO Office of Public Health and
  Environmental Hazards - 202-273-8575, 8567
  - VACO Pharmacy Benefits Management - 708-
  786-7886

Review Date
(NAME)
Chief, (SERVICE NAME)
Attachment:
    Key Activity Management Tool/Structure

Appendix G
Risk Communication Resources

1. Department of Health and Human Services
   http://www.pandemicflu.gov/rcommunication/

   "Message maps" are risk communication tools used to convey complex information, and to make it easier to understand. Each primary message has three supporting messages that can be used to provide context for the subject of the primary message.

   http://www.pandemicflu.gov/rcommunication/ pre_event_maps.pdf

2. Association of State and Territorial Health Officials
   http://www.astho.org/?template=risk_ communication.html

3. Substance Abuse and Mental Health Services Administration
   http://www.riskcommunication.samhsa.gov/ index.htm

4. World Health Organization
   http://www.who.int/csr/resources/publications/ WHO_CDS_2005_31/en/
   http://www.who.int/infectious-disease-news/IDdocs/whocds200528/whocds200528en.pdf
   http://www.who.int/csr/don/Handbook_
   influenza_pandemic_dec05.pdf

Appendix G-1
Risk and Crisis Communication:
77 Questions Commonly Asked by Journalists During a Crisis

(Reproduced with permission from: Covello, V.T., "Risk Communication and Message Mapping: A New Tool for Communicating Effectively in Public Health Emergencies and Disasters," Journal of Emergency Management, Vol.#4 No.#3, 25-40 (2006)).

Journalists are likely to ask six questions in a crisis (who, what, where, when, why, how) that relate to three broad topics: (1) What happened?; (2) What caused it to happen?; (3) What does it mean?

Specific questions include:

1. What is your name and title?
2. What are your job responsibilities?
3. What are your qualifications?
4. Can you tell us what happened?
5. When did it happen?
6. Where did it happen?
7. Who was harmed?
8. How many people were harmed?
9. Are those that were harmed getting help?
10. How certain are you about this information?
11. How are those who were harmed getting help?
12. Is the situation under control?
13. How certain are you that the situation is under control?
14. Is there any immediate danger?
15. What is being done in response to what happened?
16. Who is in charge?
17. What can we expect next?
18. What are you advising people to do?
19. How long will it be before the situation returns to normal?
20. What help has been requested or offered from others?
21. What responses have you received?
22. Can you be specific about the types of harm that occurred?
23. What are the names of those who were harmed?
24. Can we talk to them?
25. How much damage occurred?
26. What other damage may have occurred?
27. How certain are you about damages?
28. How much damage do you expect?
29. What are you doing now?
30. Who else is involved in the response?
31. Why did this happen?
32. What was the cause?
33. Did you have any forewarning that this might happen?
34. Why wasn't this prevented from happening?
35. What else could go wrong?
36. If you are not sure of the cause, what is your best guess?
37. Who caused this to happen?
38. Who is to blame?
39. Could this have been avoided?
40. Do you think those involved handled the situation well enough?
41. When did your response to this begin?
42. When were you notified that something had happened?
43. Who is conducting the investigation?
44. What are you going to do after the investigation?
45. What have you found out so far?
46. Why was more not done to prevent this from happening?
47. What is your personal opinion?
48. What are you telling your own family?
49. Are all those involved in agreement?
50. Are people overreacting?
51. Which laws are applicable?
52. Has anyone broken the law?
53. How certain are you that mistakes have not been made?
54. Have you told us everything you know?
55. What are you telling us?
56. What effects will this have on the people involved?
57. What precautionary measures were taken?
58. Do you accept responsibility for what happened?
59. Has this ever happened before?
60. Can this happen elsewhere?
61. What is the worst case scenario?
62. What lessons were learned?
63. Were those lessons implemented? Are they being implemented now?
64. What can be done to prevent this from happening again?
65. What would you like to say to those who have been harmed and to their families?
66. Is there any continuing danger?
67. Are people out of danger? Are people safe?
68. Will there be inconvenience to employees or to the public?
69. How much will all this cost?
70. Are you able and willing to pay the costs?
71. Who else will pay the costs?
72. When will we find out more?
73. What steps need to be taken to avoid a similar event?
74. Have these steps already been taken?
75. If not, why not?
76. Why should we trust you?
77. What does this all mean?

Appendix H
Sample Supply Checklists For Pandemic Planning

Appendix H-1
Examples of Consumable and Durable Supply Needs
Reproduced and modified from the HHS Pandemic Influenza Plan Supplement 3 Health Care Planning, Box 2.

- Consumable resources
  - Hand hygiene supplies (antimicrobial soap and alcohol-based, waterless hand hygiene products)
  - Disposable N95 respirators, surgical and procedure masks
  - Face shields (disposable or reusable)
  - Gowns
  - Gloves
  - Facial tissues
  - Central line kits
  - Morgue packs
- Durable resources
  - Ventilators
  - Respiratory care equipment
  - Beds
  - IV pumps

http://www.hhs.gov/pandemicflu/plan/sup3.html

Appendix H-2
Suggested Inventory of Durable and Consumable Supplies for Veterans Administration Health Care Facilities during a Pandemic Influenza
Reproduced with permission from Department of Veterans Affairs, VA Pandemic Plan

Durable resources

- Mechanical ventilators
- Manual resuscitators (bag-valve mask)
- Beds
- Stretchers/gurneys
- IV pumps
- Positive air purifying respirators (PAPRs) or other equivalent respirators

Consumable resources (consider stockpiling a 4-week supply)

- Hand hygiene supplies (antimicrobial soap and alcohol-based [>60%], waterless hand hygiene gels or foams)
- Disposable fit-testable N95 respirators

- Elastomeric respirators with P100 filters
- Surgical and procedure-type masks
- Goggles
- Gowns
- Gloves
- Facial tissues
- Central line kit
- Morgue packs
- IV equipment
- Syringes and needles for vaccine administration
- Respiratory care equipment
  - Portable oxygen
  - Regulators and flow meters
  - Oxygen and ventilator tubing, cannulae, masks
  - Endotracheal tubes, various sizes
  - Suction kits
  - Tracheotomy
  - Vacuum gauges for suction and portable suction machines
- Intensive care unit (ICU) monitoring equipment

Medications (consider stockpiling a 4-week supply)

- Nonsteroidal anti-inflammatory drugs (NSAIDs), pill and liquid forms
- Acetaminophen (pill, suppository, liquid)
- Antibiotics (consider ciprofloxacin, levofloxacin po and iv, vancomycin, piperacillin/tazobactam, ceftriaxone)
- Antivirals (oseltamivir)
- Vaccines (pandemic and seasonal influenza, pneumococcal)
- Vasopressors
- Benzodiazepines, propofol
- Proton pump inhibitors
- Bronchodilators

Items to consider including in home care kits

- Thermometers
- NSAIDs or acetaminophen
- Cough suppressants
- Oral rehydration mix packs
- Surgical or procedure-type masks for the patient to wear around others and for care providers to wear around the patient
- Printed home care instructions, including VA facility contact information and information about symptoms that should prompt the patient to see a healthcare provider

OSHA Assistance

OSHA can provide extensive help through a variety of programs, including technical assistance about effective safety and health programs, state plans, workplace consultations, and training and education.

Safety and Health Program Management System Guidelines

Effective management of worker safety and health protection is a decisive factor in reducing the extent and severity of work-related injuries and illnesses and their related costs. In fact, an effective safety and health management system forms the basis of good worker protection, can save time and money, increase productivity and reduce employee
injuries, illnesses and related workers' compensation costs.

To assist employers and workers in developing effective safety and health management system, OSHA published recommended Safety and Health Program Management Guidelines (54 Federal Register (16): 3904-3916, January 26, 1989). These voluntary guidelines can be applied to all places of employment covered by OSHA.

The guidelines identify four general elements critical to the development of a successful safety and health management system:

- Management leadership and worker involvement,
- Worksite analysis,
- Hazard prevention and control, and
- Safety and health training.

The guidelines recommend specific actions, under each of these general elements, to achieve an effective safety and health management system. The Federal Register notice is available online at www.osha.gov.

State Programs

The *Occupational Safety and Health Act of 1970* (OSH Act) encourages states to develop and operate their own job safety and health plans. OSHA approves and monitors these plans. Twenty-four states, Puerto Rico and the Virgin Islands currently operate approved state plans: 22 cover both private and public (state and local government) employment; Connecticut, New Jersey, New York and the Virgin Islands cover the public sector only. States and territories with their own OSHA-approved occupational safety and health plans must adopt standards identical to, or at least as effective as, the Federal OSHA standards.

Consultation Services

Consultation assistance is available on request to employers who want help in establishing and main-
taining a safe and healthful workplace. Largely funded by OSHA, the service is provided at no cost to the employer. Primarily developed for smaller employers with more hazardous operations, the consultation service is delivered by state governments employing professional safety and health consultants. Comprehensive assistance includes an appraisal of all mechanical systems, work practices, and occupational safety and health hazards of the workplace and all aspects of the employer's present job safety and health program. In addition, the service offers assistance to employers in developing and implementing an effective safety and health program. No penalties are proposed or citations issued for hazards identified by the consultant. OSHA provides consultation assistance to the employer with the assurance that his or her name and firm and any information about the workplace will not be routinely reported to OSHA enforcement staff. For more information concerning consultation assistance, see OSHA's website at www.osha.gov.

Strategic Partnership Program

OSHA's Strategic Partnership Program helps encourage, assist and recognize the efforts of partners to eliminate serious workplace hazards and achieve a high level of worker safety and health. Most strategic partnerships seek to have a broad impact by building cooperative relationships with groups of employers and workers. These partnerships are voluntary relationships between OSHA, employers, worker representatives, and others (e.g., trade unions, trade and professional associations, universities, and other government agencies).

For more information on this and other agency programs, contact your nearest OSHA office, or visit OSHA's website at www.osha.gov.

OSHA Training and Education

OSHA area offices offer a variety of information services, such as technical advice, publications, audiovisual aids and speakers for special engagements. OSHA's Training Institute in Arlington Heights, IL, provides basic and advanced courses in safety and health for Federal and state compliance officers, state consultants, Federal agency personnel, and private sector employers, workers and their representatives.

The OSHA Training Institute also has established OSHA Training Institute Education Centers to address the increased demand for its courses from the private sector and from other federal agencies. These centers are colleges, universities, and nonprofit organizations that have been selected after a competition for participation in the program.

OSHA also provides funds to nonprofit organizations, through grants, to conduct workplace training and education in subjects where OSHA believes there is a lack of workplace training. Grants are awarded annually.

For more information on grants, training and education, contact the OSHA Training Institute, Directorate of Training and Education, 2020 South Arlington Heights Road, Arlington Heights, IL 60005, (847) 297-4810, or see Training on OSHA's website at www.osha.gov. For further information on any OSHA program, contact your nearest OSHA regional office listed at the end of this publication.

Information Available Electronically

OSHA has a variety of materials and tools available on its website at www.osha.gov. These include electronic tools, such as Safety and Health Topics, eTools, Expert Advisors; regulations, directives and publications; videos and other information for employers and workers. OSHA's software programs and eTools walk you through challenging safety and health issues and common problems to find the best solutions for your workplace.

OSHA Publications

OSHA has an extensive publications program. For a listing of free items, visit OSHA's website at www.osha.gov or contact the OSHA Publications Office, U.S. Department of Labor, 200 Constitution Avenue, NW, N-3101, Washington, DC 20210; telephone (202) 693-1888 or fax to (202) 693-2498.

Contacting OSHA

To report an emergency, file a complaint, or seek OSHA advice, assistance, or products, call (800) 321-OSHA or contact your nearest OSHA Regional or Area office listed at the end of this publication. The teletypewriter (TTY) number is (877) 889-5627.

Written correspondence can be mailed to the nearest OSHA Regional or Area Office listed at the end of this publication or to OSHA's national office at: U.S. Department of Labor, Occupational Safety and Health Administration, 200 Constitution Avenue, N.W., Washington, DC 20210.

By visiting OSHA's website at www.osha.gov, you can also:
- File a complaint online,
- Submit general inquiries about workplace safety and health electronically, and
- Find more information about OSHA and occupational safety and health.

(OOC 5/2009)

OSHA Regional Offices

Region I
(CT,* ME, MA, NH, RI, VT*)
JFK Federal Building, Room E340
Boston, MA 02203
(617) 565-9860

Region II
(NJ,* NY,* PR,* VI*)
201 Varick Street, Room 670
New York, NY 10014
(212) 337-2378

Region III
(DE, DC, MD,* PA, VA,* WV)
The Curtis Center
170 S. Independence Mall West
Suite 740 West
Philadelphia, PA 19106-3309
(215) 861-4900

Region IV
(AL, FL, GA, KY,* MS, NC,* SC,* TN*)
61 Forsyth Street, SW, Room 6T50
Atlanta, GA 30303
(404) 562-2300

Region V
(IL, IN,* MI,* MN,* OH, WI)
230 South Dearborn Street
Room 3244
Chicago, IL 60604
(312) 353-2220

Region VI
(AR, LA, NM,* OK, TX)
525 Griffin Street, Room 602
Dallas, TX 75202
(972) 850-4145

Region VII
(IA,* KS, MO, NE)
Two Pershing Square
2300 Main Street, Suite 1010
Kansas City, MO 64108
(816) 283-8745

Region VIII
(CO, MT, ND, SD, UT,* WY*)
1999 Broadway, Suite 1690
PO Box 46550
Denver, CO 80202-5716
(720) 264-6550

Region IX
(American Samoa, AZ,* CA,* HI,* NV,*
Northern Mariana Islands)
90 7th Street, Suite 18-100
San Francisco, CA 94103
(415) 625-2547

Region X
(AK,* ID, OR,* WA*)
1111 Third Avenue, Suite 715
Seattle, WA 98101-3212
(206) 553-5930

  * These states and territories operate their own OSHA-approved job safety and health programs and cover state and local government employees as well as private sector employees. The Connecticut, New Jersey, New York and Virgin Islands plans cover public employees only. States with approved programs must have standards that are identical to, or at least as effective as, the Federal OSHA standards.

  Note: To get contact information for OSHA Area Offices, OSHA-approved State Plans and OSHA Consultation Projects, please visit us online at www.osha.gov or call us at 1-800-321-OSHA.

www.ingramcontent.com/pod-product-compliance
Lightning Source LLC
Chambersburg PA
CBHW081548170526
45166CB00009B/2618